W9-ATY-594

THE FILMS OF

Merchant Ivory

Sep, 23 /96
Bookseller Row LtD.
2445 N. Lincoln Av,
Chicago Il, 60614

Ryoichi Miyake

THE FILMS OF
Merchant Ivory

Robert Emmet Long

Harry N. Abrams, Inc., Publishers, New York

This book is dedicated to Carolyn Long

Editor: Mark Greenberg
Designer: Dirk Luykx

Library of Congress Cataloging-in-Publication Data
Long, Robert Emmet.
    The films of Merchant Ivory / Robert Emmet Long.
    208 p. 28.6 × 22.6 cm.
    Includes bibliographical references (p. 194) and index.
    ISBN 0-8109-3618-6 (cloth)
    1. Merchant Ivory Productions—History.   2. Ivory, James.
3. Merchant, Ismail.   4. Jhabvala, Ruth Prawer, 1927–
I. Title.
PN1999.M38L6 1991
384′.8′06573—dc20   91–304

Copyright © 1991 Merchant Ivory Productions

Published in 1991 by Harry N. Abrams, Incorporated, New York
A Times Mirror Company
All rights reserved. No part of the contents of this book may be
reproduced without the written permission of the publisher

Printed and bound in Japan

(frontispiece) Olive Chancellor (Vanessa
Redgrave) has a laugh at the expense of
her enemies—poor, pitiful men—in The
Bostonians.

(contents page) Miss Birdseye (Jessica
Tandy) and Basil Ransom (Christopher
Reeve), in the Boston Athenaeum. The
Bostonians.

CONTENTS

Preface

IN PREPARING this book on Merchant Ivory and their films, I have drawn on every research source available, but I have traveled frequently, too, to be as close as possible to the filmmakers I am writing about. In the autumn of 1989 their new movie *Mr. and Mrs. Bridge* was in production in Kansas City, and I went out to Missouri to see it being made. I wanted the close, personal experience of seeing Merchant and Ivory at work, and in this I was not disappointed. A bit of that experience seems worth sharing briefly. On the afternoon I arrived in Kansas City, I went looking for Ismail Merchant, who had staked out the production office for *Mr. and Mrs. Bridge* on the main floor of an office building in the city's Country Club Plaza section. In the office young women were busy at their desks answering telephones, but I did not see Merchant. When I asked for him, one of the women said that I had just missed him. "He just passed through like a hurricane," she said. When I caught up with him, I could see what she meant. He moves quickly, and seems to be everywhere.

But before catching up with him, I went out to the shooting location, further out in the Country Club district, at a large white frame house with a strong atmosphere of upper-middle-class notions of life that in earlier days still had a certain serenity about them. By one side of the house a small crowd of crew and technicians milled about, and among them I recognized Donald Rosenfeld, Merchant's assistant and the film's production supervisor. Rosenfeld, a young man who sports shoulder-length hair, dresses casually in blue jeans, and takes everything in stride, introduced me around. One of those I met before long was the actress-singer Gale Garnett, who concluded that I was "the historian." "Not exactly a historian," I said, but the "historian" label stuck and was what I became. Inside the house was another crowd of technicians, amid a battery of camera and elaborate lighting paraphernalia. A scene was being shot in the living room, where Joanne Woodward sat at a grand piano. Sunlight streamed through the windows (actually, strong lights mounted outside them), while logs burned cosily in the fireplace. Standing off to one side, yet very much at the center of all that was happening was James Ivory.

(preceding pages) Hullabaloo Over Georgie and Bonnie's Pictures.

Ivory, a trim, attractive man with brilliantly white, close-cropped hair, who was dressed casually in a sweater and dark gray, wide-wale corduroy slacks, is one of the least histrionic of film directors. Rather than shouting orders, he gives instructions quietly. He is a studious director, with watchful eyes that miss nothing as he stands by the camera, his finger moving musingly over his upper lip or propped under his chin. Takes of the same scene are repeated, each with a different nuance of angle or lighting or even, to some degree, of dialogue, as Ivory waits for the planned or unplanned moment to become "real."

I talk to Ivory and to other people both on and off the set. I have a long conversation with twenty-year-old Robert Sean Leonard, who plays the Bridges' son Douglas (later in New York I will see him in an Off-Broadway play and notice that the Newmans are also in the audience). In a room off the living room, where more of Joanne Woodward's scenes are being shot, I introduce myself to Evan Connell, author of the Bridge novels and in Kansas City as an "unofficial" script consultant. I ask him questions about the novels and the filming of them. Connell—a tall, striking, hawkfaced man—describes his father, an eye surgeon with a large and successful practice, on whom Mr. Bridge to some extent was based. He remarks on the way that Paul Newman has somehow come to look like him. At lunch time, a journalist from *Connoisseur* magazine interviews Ivory, and a camera crew is also present, shooting a documentary on the making of *Mr. and Mrs. Bridge*.

It seems like a gathering of the clan when Richard Robbins, who composes the music for Merchant Ivory films, arrives by car from New York with Ruth Prawer Jhabvala. On the evening of their arrival, a buffet dinner is served at the home of Barbara Zimmermann, Evan Connell's sister; and Merchant, Ivory, Jhabvala, and others from the set are there. Joanne Woodward sits in a chair by the fireplace wearing her husband's red baseball cap, as she samples Merchant's freshly cooked perch. Paul Newman, in a bright yellow sweat shirt, sits cross-legged on the floor next to her, drinking Michelob from a bottle, and talks to a young couple about racing cars, politics, the environment. Food is abundant not only here but also on the set, or just off the set: it is one of Merchant Ivory's trademarks. The carriage house in the rear of the Bridge house has been stocked with all manner of refreshments for the crew, and in mid-afternoons a catered luncheon is served on the main floor of a large, empty house across the street, where just about everyone eats together, from the director down to fledgling apprentice. A spirit of democracy prevails, and among the crew there is a great deal of camaraderie. Some of them have worked on Merchant Ivory pictures before and are doing so again, although they could be making larger salaries with a big Hollywood production. One production assistant I talked to, a young man from the north of London named Tom Freeman, has been a crewman on Merchant Ivory movies since, at sixteen, he went out with them to India to work on *Heat and Dust.*

One of my most durable impressions was of Ismail Merchant on my last day in Kansas City. Although at the production office part of the time, he would often be at the set, sometimes conducting men in business suits on some (to us obscure) point of business. At other times he would be on the telephone in the kitchen of the Bridge house, dealing with an array of problems that had come up. He was on the phone that evening after a ten-hour day, yet showed no sign of fatigue. Before long he suggested that I join him to see the rushes of their recent shooting. I rode in a car that followed his, first to pick up Mrs. Jhabvala, and then to drive on to the screening room in a building across town. Merchant drives with purpose and determination, picking up speed and distance with racing-car suddenness. Then the screening room: chiefly scenes in brilliant color of Newman and Woodward, and a striking sequence in which, their laughter heard first, a car full of girls appears over the rise of a hill through the yellow boughs of autumn trees. Very much an Ivory moment. Before long we hurry on across town to the premiere of the three-week Merchant Ivory retrospective at the Tivoli Theatre in the Westport section. At the crowded art-house theater, Merchant speaks to the audience with enthusiasm, and *Shakespeare Wallah* is shown. Merchant then drives off with Mrs. Jhabvala, bound on other missions, moving not quite like a hurricane perhaps but determinedly and swiftly.

While preparing this book, I have often been conscious of *Mr. and Mrs. Bridge.* I saw it come into being and watched it evolve over the course of time. Later in New York, I attended a screening of an hour of scenes from the movie; saw it announced as a coming attraction in movie houses; went to two private screenings after it had been edited (at one Gale Garnett was present and greeted me, saying "Oh, yes, you're the historian"); and saw it again on its release in the theaters. I belonged to the film, it seemed, and it belonged to me.

The preparation of this book has involved over a year and a half of work that began with my reading of Ruth Prawer Jhabvala's fiction, followed by months of consulting research sources (including Merchant Ivory's own clipping files and the files of material on Merchant Ivory at the Library of the Performing Arts at Lincoln Center). I collected approximately two thousand pages of material about the company that had to be sorted, sifted, and condensed in the form of notes. I also interviewed many people who knew them well or worked with them or had written about them. Those I interviewed include Vanessa Redgrave, Christopher Reeve, Madhur Jaffrey, Richard Robbins, Simon Callow, Walter Lassally, Annette Insdorf, Andrew Sarris, Cyrus S. H. Jhabvala, Bill O'Connell (Merchant's assistant in the early through mid-1980s and now a New York publicist), Anthony Korner (an associate of Merchant Ivory's in the early period and now publisher of *Artforum* magazine), and Maura Moynihan. *The Wandering Company,* John Pym's brief, witty monograph, was especially useful, but apart from it, surprisingly, this is the only book yet published on the film career of Merchant Ivory. Within limits, I have attempted to be comprehensive and to shed some light on the nature of the Merchant Ivory collaboration, an extraordinary venture in independent filmmaking that spans three decades and three continents. I have attempted to be objective but have not tried at all to curtail my enthusiasm for Merchant Ivory's films.

Robert Emmet Long
November 1990

Acknowledgments

THE AUTHOR wishes to express grateful appreciation to Merchant Ivory as well as to the following: Howard Batchelor, Mary Bennett, Albert Blissert, Simon Callow, John Henry Cleveland III, Vineta Colby, Evan S. Connell, John W. Crowley, Geraldine Forbes, Mark Greenberg, Annette Insdorf, Madhur Jaffrey, C. H. S. Jhabvala, Anthony Korner, Walter Lassally, Robert Sean Leonard, Dirk Luykx, William Fitch Mann, Maura Moynihan, Bill O'Connell, Joseph Penkala, Vanessa Redgrave, Christopher Reeve, Richard Robbins, Donald Rosenfeld, Andrew Sarris, Carl Sonn, Donald Vanouse, and Teresa Zaccagno.

The Company

Ismail Merchant outside the Gate
Cinema, London. (1974)

ISMAIL MERCHANT

THE POPULAR conception of Ismail (pronounced Is-mile, with
the first syllable stressed by most Westerners and the last by
Indians) Merchant is of a man who is always rushing to catch
a plane or talking on the telephone—or both at once—and it is at least
partly true. He travels constantly—to movie sets, to film festivals, to
Bombay and London, where Merchant Ivory has offices in addition to
those in New York. In Bombay, where the rental of Merchant Ivory
Productions camera and lighting equipment generates steady income,
Merchant encamps at the family's large flat; in London, where he fre-
quently obtains financing for his films, he stays at an apartment on
Portman Square in the center of the city. But it is New York, where he
has an apartment on the East Side, that is his home base. And in New
York, the center of his operations is an office in midtown Manhattan.

It is a relatively small office, consisting of several rooms with
unmatched pieces of furniture, the walls of which are decorated, quite
simply, with large posters of Merchant Ivory films. Telephones ring
constantly. Callers ask for their script department or their casting
department, unaware that such "departments" do not exist. Merchant
Ivory Productions is not vast like a Hollywood production company but
a compact organization where all the work gets done by a modest-sized

This began as a necessity. We needed someone—anyone—to cross in the background of a shot. I looked around, saw no one likely, and then Ismail, more to hurry me up than to get on screen, said he'd do it. So, like some of his future stars, he started out as an extra. His next appearance was as the theater manager in *Shakespeare Wallah* who appropriates a seat near his guest of honor, the film star Manjula, in her box at *Othello.* In *The Guru* he had a real part as the MC at a beauty contest, and by *Bombay Talkie* things had proceeded to the point where his is the first face we see, in a close-up in the very first shot: he played the producer of the big dance number being staged on a giant red typewriter. His most fiery (and perhaps most true-to-life) moments as an actor were in *Hullabaloo over Georgie and Bonnie's Pictures,* in which he is seen stamping with rage at bad news he's received over the unreliable Indian long-distance telephone. He was miscast as a peasant in *Heat and Dust* but then next turns up splendidly draped in a costly Indian shawl at the Lower East Side opening of Stash Stosz's one-man show in *Slaves of New York.* JI

We established our New York office in 1965 but didn't set up an English one until 1982, when we made *Heat and Dust,* our first film produced out of a London headquarters. For a while during that film we camped in the package room of the publisher John Murray in Albermarle Street. Murray's is in a fine Georgian house stuffed with the memorabilia of long-departed authors: locks of Byron's hair kept in drawers along with his little boots, Queen Victoria's letters, etc. There is such a hush that if a pin drops in the basement, you hear it bang six floors above. We were there because of another of Murray's authors, Ruth Jhabvala. I truly don't know how they were able to put up with a film company in pre-production, but they were marvelously unflappable. Our London offices are now in Soho, with all the other movie companies. Since *Heat and Dust,* these have been run by Paul Bradley, a hard-nosed young Englishman, also unflappable and with the steel nerves required by an independent film company of its executives. JI

cadre. At its head is Merchant (Ivory appears sometimes but prefers to work in the quiet of his apartment), who is a whole staff unto himself. When he is away, Donald Rosenfeld keeps the office humming; but the hum becomes vibrant once Merchant reappears. Merchant is a handsome, middle-aged man who is as photogenic as his stars and, beginning with *The Householder,* has made brief appearances in his films. A volatile man of quicksilver mood changes and warm emotional tones, he is nevertheless extraordinarily self-disciplined and almost totally absorbed by his work. He presents the paradox of being intensely and deeply idealistic, and intensely and deeply practical.

Ismail Noormohamed Abdul Rehman Merchant was born in Bombay on December 25, 1936 to middle-class Muslim parents, Noormohamed and Hazrabi Rehman. (Merchant is an occupational surname that Ismail added to his own family name, Rehman, while in college.) His father was a textiles dealer in the 1940s who later had interests in motorcars and racehorses, and whose winnings at the racetrack excited and delighted his family. Merchant believes that he resembles him in "the spirit of gambling," the willingness to take risks. As president of a Bombay branch of the Muslim League, his father was also active politically. The tumultuous events of Partition in 1947 left a strong impression on young Merchant. "I still have nightmares about those riots," he said. "Our politics then centered on the feeling that, simply, the British must leave. My friends and I drove about in lorries waving banners. We grew up on slogans." When Partition came, many of Merchant's relatives immigrated to Pakistan, but his own family remained determinedly in India.

At the age of nine, while growing up in Bombay, Merchant participated in a political rally that left an impression on him forever. Because of his father's position, he was coached by a Muslim preacher, or mullah, to speak before a crowd of ten thousand Muslims at the close of the observance of the Muslim New Year, Muhurram. The speech contained references to the Partition issue that he did not fully understand, but delivered as it was by a boy, it made a vivid and stirring impression. It inflamed the crowd. Merchant relates the experience to his passionate commitment to his films. "I had stirred up that crowd," he remarks, "and there was no way I could calm it down. Now, once one of our films starts, it is like that crowd, there is no going back, no stopping. I knew I could move that crowd and I know I can finish the film. This is the attitude I have always adopted."

Bombay was also the center of the Indian film industry, which attracted its own crowds and, before long, the interest of Merchant. In 1949, he met the film actress Nimmi, and was entranced by her and her life. Nimmi's mother and Merchant's parents made annual visits to the same saint's shrine at Ajmere, and although they were not acquainted, they knew some people in common. One day on a visit to Bombay, Nimmi paid a call at the Merchant house. Thereafter Nimmi, who was in her twenties, and Merchant, who was thirteen, became very close. "She took me," Merchant says, "as a companion and younger brother.

She would take me to the studios (there were some twenty-five in Bombay) and say 'You must become a star.'"

Merchant was educated in schools in Bombay, attending both Jesuit and Muslim secondary schools and, beginning in 1954, the Jesuit-run St. Xavier's College. That he should have gone to Jesuit schools was not surprising. They were not strictly denominational and did not proselytize; rather, they offered the best available education in English. His parents were ambitious for him as their only son (he had six sisters, three older and three younger), and his father hoped that he would enter one of the professions, become a doctor or barrister. At an early age, however, he already knew that he had a calling in films. Even in secondary school, he staged variety shows that featured dance, music, and drama. At St. Xavier's College he studied political science and English literature among other subjects, "but you know," he remarked, "I spent most of my time in the canteen, planning our variety shows." Exhibiting a flair for showmanship, he persuaded the head of the college to allow him to stage them in the Quadrangle, where they attracted more attention. Throughout this time he went constantly to films, including ones from Hollywood, and began to set his sights on going to America to produce films with mixed Indian and Hollywood casts. The earnings of his previous variety shows had gone to the college, but his final one (he graduated in 1958), a benefit, provided the funds that were to take him to New York and pay his tuition for the MBA course in business administration at New York University, for which he had just been accepted.

The courses Merchant took at NYU at night did not interest him greatly, but he breezed through them. He spent part of his time at concerts, discovering Western music, and going frequently to films, which also brought new revelations. In India he did not have the opportunity to see the films of the Bengali director Satyajit Ray, but discovered them instead in New York, as well as the work of the great European filmmakers who emerged after World War II. "It changed my opinion of all those Hollywood films," he remarked. "Snap, like that. Suddenly, it was Ray, Bergman, De Sica, Fellini; I went avidly to their films. I continued to go to Hollywood films, but the European films became a passion. De Sica affected me greatly. I loved Bergman's *Smiles of a Summer Night*."

In 1958 Merchant lived at International House at the northwestern edge of the Columbia University campus, and worked as a messenger for the Indian delegation to the United Nations, where he began to make contacts and attempted to recruit backers for the entertainment projects he envisioned. A number of articles about him claim that he posed as the Indian delegate, or was announced as the delegate, perhaps jokingly, by a U.N. receptionist; and I asked him if this was true. "I never posed as the Indian delegate," he said, "but I was always announced as the Indian delegate because the receptionist had taken a great fancy to me. She would always announce me as the Indian delegate."

On the porch of Ismail Merchant's Hudson Valley house. (1989)

Had Ismail been brought up in Calcutta instead of Bombay, this would not have been the case. Ray's films, made in the Bengali language, were not ordinarily shown outside West Bengal: to have been commercially viable in the rest of India, they would have required subtitles in the many, many Indian languages, as well as in English. This situation has never changed; there has never been an "art house" circuit in India for subtitled movies, whether Ray's or European ones. JI

14

After several months at the U.N., Merchant took a job as an account executive trainee at the McCann-Erickson advertising agency, another opportunity to make contacts since the company had ties with television production in New York. He courted people assiduously and, among others, came to meet Madhur and Saeed Jaffrey, who were acting in New York and were later to become veteran performers in Merchant Ivory films. In my interview with her, Madhur Jaffrey—a sparkling conversationalist as well as a gifted actress—recalled Merchant at that time. "He thought big," she said, "he always thought with his name on the top, as the presenter, the producer. He wanted to do things on a grand scale. At that time he said he wanted to present an Indian dancer at the Radio City Music Hall, and we said 'Ismail, are you crazy? They wouldn't want an Indian dancer at the Radio City Music Hall.' We didn't know at that time that he was quite capable of convincing people she must be seen. He did have that ability." Before long, through contacts he made at McCann-Erickson, Merchant made his first film, only 14 minutes in length, *The Creation of Woman*, a tale set to Indian dance and music inspired by a mythological story in a collection of Indian fiction that Merchant had recently read. It was narrated by Saeed Jaffrey and, although shot on a beggarly budget in a New York studio over one weekend, was surprisingly good. With the film in hand, and having just received his MBA degree at NYU (in 1990 he would be honored by the university as its "Alumnus of the Year"), Merchant quit his job at McCann-Erickson and went out to Hollywood.

Before leaving, Merchant arranged for a press release to be sent to Los Angeles announcing the impending arrival of a bigwig Indian producer: himself. "All along," Merchant remarked, "I had discovered that you didn't need money to achieve something. I had done nothing, but I was confident that I *would* do all the things that I said I had done." But if he expected the press release to excite interest in the film capital, it did not; no delegations from the studios were present to greet him when he stepped off the train. He went to work part time at a clothing store, and on the 9 PM to 4 AM shift in the classified ads department of the *Los Angeles Times*. Yet he still found time to talk himself onto the sound stages of studios, where he impressed and charmed people. Soon he met Agnes Moorhead and Susan Hayward, with whom he talked of his plans for films in India in which they would appear.

It was also on his mind at the time to secure an Academy Award nomination for *The Creation of Woman*. When the Academy informed him that his picture could not be entered for the 1961 awards because it had not played the required three days in a commercial theater in 1960, he acted quickly. He approached the owner of the Fine Arts Cinema in Los Angeles, persuading him that his short film would make an ideal companion piece to Bergman's *The Devil's Eye*. The film was booked at the cinema, ran its required three days, and was seen by enough Academy members to generate an Oscar nomination. He now had a calling card.

(left to right) Michael York, Barry Foster, and Aparna Sen, on the Ganges in a scene from *The Guru*.

After nearly a year in Hollywood, Merchant left for the Cannes Film Festival, where *The Creation of Woman* was to be screened in competition (it was to receive a strongly favorable notice in *Variety*), and with the plan of making a film, as yet unwritten, in India. En route he stopped in New York, where he was invited to a screening of *The Sword and the Flute*, a documentary on Indian miniature painting narrated by his friend Saeed Jaffrey and directed by a young American filmmaker named James Ivory, who was present at the occasion. "During our conversation that first evening," Merchant recalls of Ivory, "I realized that he knew about India not in a dry, academic way but with understanding—something I have never encountered in an American either before or since. What was absolutely extraordinary was his *feeling* for India." Ivory was then interested in a film project about life in an Indian village, which he would photograph and Sidney Meyers would direct—if money could be found to do it. Merchant soon told him that he would try to help him find the needed capital in India. In May 1961, he and Ivory also agreed to become partners in a production company that would make movies in India for a Western audience.

Merchant and Ivory met again in India in November of that year, only to suffer one setback (sufficient funding for the film Ivory and Meyers hoped to do could not be found, and the undertaking had to be abandoned) and to make a new beginning with a movie that involved a second momentous meeting—this time with Ruth Prawer Jhabvala. The project that Merchant and Ivory now decided upon was a screen adaptation of Jhabvala's novel *The Householder*, which Merchant had read in Hollywood; he had been told by a seasoned scriptwriter, Isobel Lennart, that it would make a good property for a young independent film company. In Delhi, Merchant and Ivory approached Jhabvala with a certain apprehension, since they had heard that she guarded her privacy fiercely. She *was* wary when a stranger called her on the telephone, pretending at first to be her mother-in-law, but once she'd admitted them to her house, she agreed to work with them.

Thirty years later, with extraordinary achievement behind him, Merchant is independent filmmaking's leading producer, but his expansive personality has changed hardly at all. Stories abound of his zest for work, showmanship, and outreaching sociability. I collected further stories about him from Maura Moynihan, who has appeared in two of Merchant Ivory's films, and first met Merchant in the mid-1970s when she was fifteen, and her father, Senator Daniel Patrick Moynihan, was U. S. Ambassador to India. Merchant, Ivory, and the Moynihans have since remained close, and Maura makes no bones about how fortunate she feels to have been adopted into "the Merchant Ivory family." "When he loves you," she says of Merchant, "my God, he loves you." She speaks of his joie de vivre, which she calls "the greatest I've ever known, enormous, expansive. He's really the patriarch of the clan, as far as I can see." She remembers going about with him in Bombay in 1983, when he gave to beggars, opened doors for people, bought flowers, and squired about his many nieces and nephews (he has over

Like a lion-tamer with his prize lion: Ismail Merchant and Lucille Ball, photographed in Hollywood. (1960)

(opposite) Ismail Merchant with Mikki Ansin, the stills photographer of *Mr. and Mrs. Bridge*, and Richard Robbins in Kansas City. (1989)

twenty), who "hung onto his ankles and shirttails"; and she believes that it is out of the Indian family tradition that he comes by his gift for taking care of people, of "nurturing" them.

A devout Muslim, Merchant rises early every morning to say his prayers. He then walks his dog, or does calisthenics, or swims. Sometimes he plays tennis with Richard Robbins. His film work consumes him, but he has many interests, including music. He knows many musicians, including Ustad Vilayat Khan and Ravi Shankar, but a particularly close friend is Zakir Hussain, India's premier tabla player. "Ismail's great passion," Robbins told me, "is Indian classical music, but he also goes to Western recitals and is very excited by them." He is also fond of poetry, particularly in Urdu; speaks three languages: English, Hindi, and Urdu, and also knows, if he does not speak, Gujarati, Marathi, and Persian. Merchant is also a great auction goer, and may be found at Christie's or Sotheby's acquiring rugs and china. "He can tell you," a friend says, "about where the latest auctions are, where you can buy a carpet, where you can get good flowers. He has this ability to remember everything and retain it in his head. He's remarkable that way."

But the most famed of his interests apart from making films is cooking. He is, in fact, the author of a highly touted cookbook, *Ismail Merchant's Indian Cuisine* (1986). Merchant began cooking in 1958 in New York as an inexpensive way to establish a congenial atmosphere for writers, actors, financiers, and others who were becoming part of his circle, and to re-create his mother's and sisters' dishes and tastes. It was in 1972, during the filming of *Savages*, when funds were tight and spirits flagging, that he began his practice of cooking once-a-week meals for cast and crew.

Richard Robbins, who claims partial credit for Merchant's cookbook, having inspired the idea and written down the recipes as he cooked, speaks of the élan with which Merchant goes shopping in Florence and Paris. "He instantly absorbs all the markets," Robbins remarks, "and knows just what local products he wants and how to combine them in his own recipes. It's an experience to go shopping with him. Soon all the vendors know him." The special feature of Merchant's cooking is the way he creates wonderful, unconventional tastes, all done with speed and economy. His cooking has never been strictly traditional Indian cuisine, but a combination of Indian with French or other local styles, an approach he calls "pragmatic and experimental, and not so different from the way I go about finding finance for my films."

But whether cooking or collecting rugs, Merchant is ever mindful of business. Before any film venture can be launched, Jhabvala and Ivory must first win Merchant over; but once persuaded, he goes out to find funding with steely determination. "If I call someone and he doesn't call me back," Merchant comments, "I'm not going to get upset about it. I'll call him back ten times if I have to. I'll speak with the secretary and charm her into calling me by my first name. Eventually,

In New York we had to go into Sotheby's once with Ernest Vincze, the cameraman of *Jane Austen in Manhattan*, who needed to look over the main sales room so he could light it for an upcoming scene in that film. There was a sale of Oriental carpets going on, with some very spirited bidding. To my horror, I saw Ismail had his hand up, and he kept it in the air until the gavel banged down, whereupon one of the courtly black attendants who then circulated in the sales rooms during auctions at Sotheby's—holdovers from the more genteel days of Parke Bernet—appeared at his elbow with a little book for him to sign. As decisive at auctions as in other places, Ismail has a very good eye for silver and metalwork, porcelain and rugs. It's tempting to think this aesthetic is as much of the blood as the eye. Like the nomad ancestors he claims, moving forever over Asia's plains and through mountain passes, he would be able easily to carry away his valuables in a hurry. JI

I'll get to the boss." A colleague says of Merchant: "He's like an elephant outside the financier's door. You can see him through the glass, you cannot shift him, he won't go away, he is very patient, and there is always the chance that he will come crashing in."

A tough businessman, Merchant imposes the strictest austerities on his productions: money invested in them goes not for inflated salaries but onto the screen. He often defers much of his own salary and is always the last to be paid, and he persuades well-known stars to appear in his films for considerably less than their usual salaries, offering the inducement of quality movies by which they would like to be remembered. And rather than paying for props, he is a constant, and often flamboyant, borrower. For *The Deceivers*, he needed a cache of jewelry that would cost a third of his total budget, but was unfazed. "I went to the Gem Palace, a wonderful jewelry shop in Jaipur," he remarks, "and asked if I could perhaps borrow a bit of jewelry for the film. The Kasliwal brothers, the owners, filled up two old briefcases with about $2 million worth of jewels, many of them uncut stones, and brought them, without any form of security, to the set, which ended up looking like Aladdin's cave."

Jhabvala and Ivory complement Merchant in a way that gives creative interplay to their collaboration. "I think that in many ways," Madhur Jaffrey comments, "Ismail was very, very lucky to fall in with Ruth and Jim, who have wonderful taste and sense of style, and they were able to marry that with Ismail's ability to sell anything. I think it wasn't quite clear when I first met him what he was going to be selling. It was going to be in the film world or in the entertainment world because that was what was most glamorous to him as a child growing up in Bombay. But what shape it would take he wasn't quite sure, and he didn't quite take off until he met Jim and Ruth, and then it took a form, and it was very good for him because they curtailed him in a wonderful way, so that his energy has been used to make good films." But she also points out that the role Merchant has played in the collaboration has been important for Jhabvala and Ivory, too. "I think both Jim and Ruth are retiring," she remarks, "and not really able to push themselves on their own, but allied with Ismail they can push themselves to their fullest capacity."

Perhaps the key point to make about Merchant is that he is a master at persuasion. He can make people believe in him, convince investors that they must have whatever film he makes. To quote Madhur Jaffrey again: "He's a sort of trader-salesman of the cleverest sort. Most people would love to have that ability, which requires all sorts of things, a certain fixated quality, an understanding of human nature, and much else. I don't know how he does it, and why he is successful at it and other people aren't, but he has *tremendous* energy. No one, I think, has as much energy as Ismail." Few people can resist Merchant in his ebullience, when, a smile suddenly blooming on his face, he exclaims:

"Call me Ismail."

There are some props you can *only* borrow; prop-hire houses don't always stock the kinds of things needed in films. Merchant Ivory is not the only borrower, or a borrower solely out of low-budget necessity. In *Mr. and Mrs. Bridge*, where would we find Boy Scout Merit badge sashes from the 1940s, for example, unless we borrowed them from the original owners. We were happy to discover that they had also carefully saved their balsa-wood-and-tissue-paper model airplanes. JI

Let me add that, as an independent producer, you have to be a master of survival as well. No one wants to pay you the money owed to you: they want to use your money for the maximum period of time for their own purposes, thereby earning interest on it. Strange charges are applied to your film's earnings, and in auditing you sometimes find these charges are for gifts given to you by your distributors for Christmas or New Year. Executives buy suits from Armani and charge them to your quarterly report. You have to have an eagle's-eye watch on them all the time.

In the same way, your film is not finished after you complete it. You must be involved in promotion, exhibition, public relations—you continue to work for your films for years. A 10 percent portion of the film's income slowly begins to trickle your way. And even for that amount, you must expect threats, lawsuits, and shouting matches. Well, this is acceptable to me, as my passion is to make movies, and movies of substance and quality. I now see all of our films playing everywhere in the world, and so our struggles to survive for these thirty years have been well worth it. IM

Ruth Jhabvala in the palace at
Bikaner in Rajasthan, India, during
a location-scouting expedition for
The Guru. (1967)

RUTH PRAWER JHABVALA

C. S. H. Jhabvala—"Jhab"—in a charac-
teristic pose, with Ruth, in Benares
during filming of *The Guru.* (1967)

ONE MORNING during the Christmas season in New York,
I called at the apartment of Ruth Prawer Jhabvala. Her building in Manhattan's East 50s is in a sense a Merchant Ivory
compound, since Merchant, Ivory, and Jhabvala all have apartments
there, and their mornings frequently begin with breakfast at the Jhab-
valas; they are like a family. I had talked to Mrs. Jhabvala previously,
and was now calling to meet her husband, Cyrus, who had flown from
Delhi to spend time with his wife. He greeted me at the door and soon
was serving coffee as we talked in the living room. From a further
room came the sound of typewriter keys tapping in a steady tattoo:
Mrs. Jhabvala at work on a manuscript.

Cyrus Jhabvala—slender, pleasant appearing, and in his late
sixties—is the most agreeable of men. To his friends he is known as
"Jhab" (pronounced "Job"). His conversation, relaxed and unhurried, is
often accompanied by a grin, for he is celebrated within the Merchant
Ivory circle for his wit, which can be astute and tends to be very sly as
well as wry. Before long I find myself laughing, perhaps more often
and louder than I should and thus disturbing Mrs. Jhabvala at her

work. Jhabvala recalls his first meeting with Merchant and Ivory: "Ismail was very young then, dazzling, only twenty-four, just a boy. Jim wasn't a great deal older. We immediately became friends. They haven't changed at all." He discounts the widely circulated legend that his wife lived in India as an almost total recluse, but he admits that they did not socialize a great deal. He himself worked a long day as a partner in a successful architectural firm in New Delhi and later also taught at a college of architecture there.

In 1976, after twenty-four years in India, their children having grown to adulthood, Ruth Jhabvala made the decision to move to New York. She needed, at this point in her life, to live away from India; her husband has stood by her and supported her. In an unusual arrangement, she spends the winters with Jhab in Delhi, and he comes several times a year to New York to be with her. "We've given most of our money," he says, "to airlines and telephone companies." In New York, Ruth Jhabvala leads a retiring life but is never entirely alone. She is very close to Merchant and Ivory and has other friends. And for part of the year at least there is Jhab, who has recently retired from his architectural practice, spends part of his time painting (some of his paintings are reproduced on the jackets of the new uniform edition of Ruth Jhabvala's books), and is preparing a book—a collection of his drawings of the views and historic architecture of Delhi (much of it now in ruins), accompanied by his text.

Ruth Prawer (prah'-ver) Jhabvala (job'-va-la) was born on May 7, 1927 in Cologne, Germany, the daughter of Marcus Prawer, a Jewish solicitor who had fled Poland during World War I to avoid military conscription. Her mother, Eleanora Cohn, came from Berlin, of forefathers who had also fled conscription in Poland and Russia. In "Disinheritance," her talk before the Scottish Arts Council on the occasion of receiving its Neil Gunn Fellowship, Jhabvala described her early years and later life abroad: "I was born," she remarked, "into what seemed a very solidly based family who had identified strongly with the Germany around them—had been through the 1914–18 War with them—had sung for the Kaiser and the fatherland." Her maternal grandfather was the cantor in the biggest synagogue in Cologne, a man who prided himself on being a well-regarded citizen and whose friendships included Christian pastors. There were many aunts and uncles, "all well settled, all German patriots, full of bourgeois virtues and pleasures." These memories belong to Jhabvala's earliest years, up to 1933. In 1933, when Hitler became chancellor of Germany, all this changed suddenly and tragically.

In the Neil Gunn lecture, Jhabvala acknowledged that she had never before talked about the period in her life between 1933 and 1939, her years between six and twelve—had, in fact, wiped them from her memory. Beginning in 1933, book burnings began, and the deprivation of many Jews of their professional livelihoods. In 1935 the Nuremberg Laws were passed, forbidding marriages (and sexual relations) between Jews and German "nationals." In 1938 came mass arrests of Jews, who

Vanessa Redgrave and Madeleine Potter in *The Bostonians.*

20

were sent to concentration camps, particularly those at Dachau and Buchenwald. In November of that year, after a Jew shot a German official in Paris, an orgy of Jew-hating violence occurred on an unprecedented scale. In a twenty-four-hour period, tens of thousands of Jewish shops and homes were broken into by stormtroopers, and nearly two hundred synagogues burned; the Nazis were to call this mass violence the *Kristallnacht*, or "night of broken glass." It was followed by the deportation to concentration camps of more than thirty thousand Jews—one in ten of those who remained in Germany. The Prawers, who lived through all of this, escaped deportation to the camps because—due to Ruth's father—they were Polish nationals. They managed to make their way to England in April 1939.

For several months, as part of the British scheme to evacuate children, Ruth and her brother Siegbert, two years older, stayed with two maiden sisters in Coventry, then joined their parents in Hendon, a northern suburb of London, where the father bought a house and began to make his livelihood in the clothing business. From 1940 to 1945, Ruth attended the Hendon County School where, barely in her teens, she wrote fiction constantly. She had been writing even in Germany, almost as soon as she learned the alphabet; now she learned English immediately and wrote in her adopted language about English subjects, especially the lower middle classes. "I wrote about them," she said, "in the stories, plays, unfinished novels that I turned out in a relentless stream all through those school years."

She also read a great deal. "Not really having a world of my own," she remarked, "I made up for my disinheritance by absorbing the world of others. The more regional, the more deeply rooted a writer was, the more I loved them: George Eliot, Thomas Hardy, Charles Dickens. Their landscapes, their childhood memories became mine. I adopted them passionately. But I was equally passionate to adopt, for instance, the landscapes of Marcel Proust, of James Joyce, of Henry James, of the great Russians—Tolstoy, Dostoevsky, Turgenev, Chekhov (that noble roll call). It was as if I had no senses of my own— besides no country of my own—but only theirs."

From 1945 to 1951, Ruth studied English literature at Queen Mary College, London University, where she wrote her MA thesis, "The Short Story in England." In 1948, while she was in college, tragedy struck the Prawer family again, when her father committed suicide. By the end of the war all of his relatives in Germany—over forty of them—were dead; and when reports came out of how people died in the concentration camps, he was overwhelmed by grief. "Suicide," Jhabvala said, "became almost an epidemic at that time." A few months after her father's death, Ruth met a young Indian architect named Cyrus S. H. Jhabvala, who had been studying at London University. A Parsee, he belonged to a Europeanized and often affluent community that came to India from Persia around the eighth century. Jhabvala was returning to India but asked Ruth to wait for him. She did. He returned two years later; they were married in June 1951 in a north

London register office and left England to make their home in the old, quiet section of New Delhi. A whole new world opened before Ruth Prawer Jhabvala, then twenty-four.

The effect of India on her, she said, "was stunning, overwhelming, beyond words. I entered a world of sensuous delights that perhaps children—other children—enter. Was it in reaction to the bleakness and deprivations of my own childhood—Nazi Germany and then wartime blitzed London (those nights and days spent in damp air-raid shelters, and queuing for matches and margarine)?" She immediately began writing fiction about India, reveling in this exotic world, immersed in it as if she were Indian herself. But after ten years passed, a new feeling about herself in relation to the country began to take hold, the consciousness that she was *not* Indian. "I was no longer immersed in sensuous delight but had to struggle against all the things people do have to struggle against in India: the tide of poverty, disease and squalor rising all around; the heat—the frayed nerves; the strange, alien, often inexplicable Indian character." After writing *Heat and Dust,* her novel about the difficult, complicated rite of passage of Westerners in India, Jhabvala reached the decision to live in New York.

Jhabvala's novels fall roughly into three periods. The early ones from *Amrita* (1956) to *A Backward Place* (1965) deal with Westernized Indian society in or around New Delhi after the country had achieved independence and the engrossing struggle to expel imperialism had been replaced by the mundane drama of living in an underdeveloped third-world country. Although knowing relatively little at first hand of middle-class Hindu family life, it became her subject and is brought to life with brilliant clarity and a sense of seeming omniscience. The great business of arranging marriages, the concern to preserve the indivisibility of the Hindu family provide the terrain of her satire and the social types she creates, with their vanity or self-deception, affectation, or moral indolence. Her characters are treated with remarkable empathy and understanding, yet their inmost natures are laid bare astringently and with a kind of universal irony.

Her second period, anticipated by her early novel *Esmond in India* (1958), can be seen in writing that includes *Travelers* (1973) and *Heat and Dust* (1975), in which she has become primarily concerned with Westerners in India, with the meeting of different cultures that characteristically brings frustration. India tends to be seen now through the eyes of the English, who are often adrift, unable to come to terms with the Subcontinent. The terrain of her novels and short stories becomes increasingly subjective and psychological. The novels of Jhabvala's most recent period come out of her residence in New York City, and are largely set there. *In Search of Love and Beauty* (1983) and *Three Continents* (1988), a large, ambitious work that left her exhausted by the time she finished it, have the abstract contours of allegorical romance reminiscent of Henry James's *The Golden Bowl* and extend the themes of her later Indian period insofar as they deal with a baffled quest for transcendence. They, too, belong to Jhabvala's vision of disinheritance.

Jennifer Kendal and Shashi Kapoor in
Bombay Talkie.

Beginning in 1961, when Merchant and Ivory called at her house and their long collaboration began, Jhabvala has managed two careers in tandem, her fiction writing and her screenwriting. At times they are interrelated, since her novels, especially the later ones, make use of cinematic techniques. Flashbacks are employed, scenes are spliced and juxtaposed with editing-room expertness. One of the most prominent features of her novel *Travelers* is that Jhabvala focuses on four Western characters in India, with events seen from the point of view of each in episodes that alternate with the effect of camera cuts. *Heat and Dust*, also set in India, uses a similar cross-cutting device but is concentrated here in two English girls divided by a generation in time. Perhaps Jhabvala's most cinematic novel is her recent *Three Continents* (a screenplay, in fact, before it became a novel), which has tense, suspenseful pacing and highlighted dramatic scenes that would hold a movie audience. The story flows forward with a strong visual sense, so that it is as if the reader were an onlooker (who knows more than the characters do themselves), as if a camera were tracking, recording all that is occurring.

But if Jhabvala's work in films has affected her fiction, her fiction has also influenced her films. Two Merchant Ivory movies, *The House-holder* and *Heat and Dust*, were adapted for the screen by Jhabvala from her own novels; but in other cases the situations and character types of her novels have entered into the conception of her original screenplays. The cinema-as-escape motif in *The Householder*, and the ending of *A Backward Place* in which Bal ("child") travels with his young English wife to Bombay, dreaming of becoming successful in films, anticipate Jhabvala and Ivory's exploration of the Bombay film world in *Bombay Talkie*. The naive Western searchers for transcendence in India appear first in her fiction and then in her films; moreover, in many cases they are young women who fall under the influence of a guru, that dubious, satirized figure who turns up recurringly in Merchant Ivory movies written by Jhabvala.

The interrelatedness of her fiction and screenwriting can be seen particularly in the way in which her screenplay of *Autobiography of a Princess* anticipates and prepares for her novel *Heat and Dust*, which, in turn, was adapted by her as a film. The sequence creates a progression from film into fiction, and then from fiction back into film. In his collaboration with her, Ivory could not have found a more trained analyst of Anglo-Indian relationships and the international theme. But whether their movies are laid in India or in Europe or America, Jhabvala has been a guiding force in the shaping of many Merchant Ivory films.

I asked Ivory how exactly he works with Jhabvala in preparing a screenplay. "It's a step-by-step thing," he said. "We decide what we want to emphasize in the script, and I tell her what my favorite scenes might well be, or are, if she's adapting a book. If it's from a book then I mark up the book, so that she knows the favorite things of mine that I wouldn't want to lose. I would want to make something of them. She usually agrees, though she doesn't always. Then she writes her script, and I never see it. I have no idea what she's doing. She's off somewhere doing it, maybe she's off in India. She comes back with this mess of papers, all scotch-taped together. Then I read it and I start shouting: 'No, no, this isn't what I wanted,' and 'Why have you left out such and such a thing?,' and 'Are you crazy?' And this will go on for an hour or two, and then we sort of redo it, with me trying to push things I want, and she agreeing to some of it. And that's it, that becomes the screenplay. And then, usually before we begin shooting, it goes through another kind of slight metamorphosis; it alters before shooting, and then it alters during the shooting."

When she is available, Jhabvala watches the film being shot (usually from afar), and makes changes in the script. Scenes that had looked good on paper turn out to be disappointing and are scrapped. An ending may be changed. A character takes on unexpected life and is given an enlarged role in the film. For the most part, one can see how Jhabvala and Ivory work together, but at a certain point their collaboration becomes harder to define because in many respects of taste and sensibility they are much alike. Both are drawn to a comedy of manners having an ironic detachment, and they have great finesse and sub-

The Begum (Madhur Jaffrey, *left*) plots with her purdah ladies in a scene from *Heat and Dust.*

Both brother and sister are passionate filmgoers—he in Oxford, where he prefers to go by himself, and Ruth in New York, most often accompanied by her husband. She sees more movies in a year than I do, and I see a lot. Though not exactly catholic in her tastes, she still manages to see a somewhat wider range of films than I do, going to the more commercial kind when I tell her that something is interesting and ought not to be missed, as well as seeking out many subtitled films that, I'm sorry to admit, I all too often skip. As children, because they were Jews, Ruth and her brother could not go to the movies in Nazi Germany, and they saw their first American films during school vacations in Holland, dubbed into Dutch. Later in India there were only Hindi song-and-dance films or the big Hollywood commercial kind, which didn't much interest her. So she dropped out, missing the French New Wave, Ingmar Bergman, and Fellini, Visconti, and Antonioni. *La Dolce Vita* did eventually make it to Delhi, though dubbed into English. But it seemed a revelation, she said, and she began going again whenever there was something to see: this was partly for pleasure, and partly also to get an idea of the various forms of narrative used in present-day moviemaking. Siegbert Prawer's response to his own movie-going wasn't to be the writing of screenplays, but a book on horror films, *Caligari's Children: The Film as Tale of Terror.* JI

tlety. At times their talents seem to merge in an almost symbiotic way.

Both Jhabvala and her brother, Siegbert, have distinguished themselves in literature. Siegbert, who writes under the name S. S. Prawer, is a noted scholar who has published numerous books on German literature. Until his recent retirement, he was Taylor Professor of German Language and Literature at Oxford University. The scope of Jhabvala's attainments is impressive. She has published ten novels and five collections of short stories, many of which first appeared in *The New Yorker* and which have placed her in the front rank of contemporary writers. At the same time, she has written fourteen of Merchant Ivory's films thus far produced (*The Householder, Shakespeare Wallah, The Guru, Bombay Talkie, Autobiography of a Princess, Roseland, Hullabaloo Over Georgie and Bonnie's Pictures, Jane Austen in Manhattan, The Europeans, Quartet, Heat and Dust, The Bostonians, A Room with a View,* and *Mr. and Mrs. Bridge*). She has also written the screenplay of *Madame Sousatzka,* the John Schlesinger film, as well as a number of plays.

Books and articles have been written about her, and she has received numerous honors and awards, including an honorary Doctor of Literature degree from her alma mater, London University. She has received both Britain's National Film Critics Award and the British Academy of Film and Television Arts Award (the English equivalent of the Oscar) for Best Screenplay for *Heat and Dust;* an Academy Award for Best Screenplay Adaptation for *A Room with a View;* and England's coveted Booker Prize for her novel *Heat and Dust.* She has been the recipient of a Guggenheim Fellowship (1976), the Neil Gunn Fellowship (1979), and a MacArthur Foundation grant (1984). It is hard to conceive of another resident screenwriter with a film company having Jhabvala's credentials.

Yet she lives in New York very quietly, and almost anonymously. Jhabvala is a slightly built woman (she is a little over five feet tall and weighs 100 pounds) in her early sixties. What one notices on first meeting her is her kindness. She is, however, not greatly given to socializing. "I grew up alone," she remarks, "and I stayed alone. I need a lot of solitude." Her mornings are taken up with her writing: "the only three hours in the day I'm really alive." Jhabvala's daughters, now in their thirties, live in different parts of the world. Renana, her eldest, is a union organizer in the Indian textile city of Ahmedabad and is married to a journalist; Ava, an architect, is married to a British architect and lives in Essex, England; and Firoza is a teacher in California, married to an American lawyer. She is in touch with all of them, but her greatest resource, Ivory remarks, "is, finally, Jhab. The months when he's not here are very barren for her." When Merchant and Ivory are away from New York, she sometimes eats alone, completely unrecognized, at one of the coffee shops on First or Second Avenue. But whether at home in the city, or staying at Ivory's house in upstate New York, she is dedicated to her ritual of writing in the morning, of perfecting her craft. "That's what I'm here for," she says.

James Ivory and Ismail Merchant in New York City. (1974)

JAMES IVORY

IN THE KITCHEN of a large house in the Hudson River Valley, on a warm summer afternoon in 1989, Ruth Jhabvala sprinkles sugar over several bowls of fresh strawberries, while James Ivory speaks of the trip to Cooperstown from which they have just returned, where he had delivered an address at Hyde Hall on the occasion of the opening of an exhibition. Here at Ivory's home, where I am paying a visit, conversation is relaxed and informal, interrupted at times by telephone calls or the arrival of someone at the door. A neighbor appears with his son, wondering if Ivory might have a role for the boy in *Mr. and Mrs. Bridge*. In the early evening a few friends stop by, and everyone gathers on the white-pillared front porch, from the broad expanse of which Franklin Roosevelt once delivered a speech. Dinner is at the rambling white frame house a short distance away of Richard Robbins, who has an open face and manner, and is one of the most popular members of the circle. After dinner the guests gather in the living room, while Robbins plays a recording of classical music. Ruth Jhabvala perches in a window seat, her hands clasped about her knees, her head back and eyes closed, listening.

Ivory bought his house, located in a rural area of Columbia County about two hours drive from New York City, in 1975. He had been looking for an investment property to replace the one in California that had been condemned for a freeway when he noticed a National Trust announcement of properties for sale that led to his discovery of the white Federal brick home, which had been built in 1805 by Jacob Rutsen Van Rensselaer, a local political boss and general in the War of 1812. Inside, prints of places from abroad associated with Merchant Ivory films decorate the walls: the Piazza Signoria in Florence from *A Room with a View*; St. Mark's Cathedral from *Venice: Theme and Vari-*

ations; the Elephanta Caves in India from *Bombay Talkie*; King's College Chapel at Cambridge from *Maurice*.

Ivory's home has been described as "a cross between an English country house and a small, informal film colony." Many of the actors in Merchant Ivory films—Shashi Kapoor, Madhur Jaffrey, Paul Newman, Joanne Woodward, Christopher Reeve, Greta Scacchi, Madeleine Potter, James Wilby, Julian Sands, and Helena Bonham Carter, among others—have visited here. At this country retreat, Merchant and Ivory work on their films and Jhabvala has a quiet sanctuary in which to work under a big maple tree, next to a pond. In the mid-1980s, Merchant and Ivory converted a farm building into an editing room; it was here that *A Room with a View, Slaves of New York,* and most recently *Ballad of the Sad Café* were edited.

People often assume that Ivory is English and are surprised to hear his American speech when they talk to him on the telephone. He was born into an upper-middle-class family in Berkeley, California on June 7, 1928. His paternal grandfather immigrated to America from Ireland in the 1870s, settling in the upstate New York town of Norwich. His father, Edward, grew up in the town, graduated from the Syracuse University School of Forestry in 1916, and then worked for a year for a lumber company in Bogalusa, Louisiana, where he met Ivory's mother, Hallie DeLoney, sixteen at the time. His mother was from an old Louisiana family whose DeLoney name would seem to imply French ancestry, but as far as has ever been determined, her family origins were actually English.

In 1917, after the United States entered World War I, Edward Ivory (who had been in ROTC in college) was called up as an officer and served with a unit in France. After the war ended, he returned to work in Thomas Edison's New Jersey "think tank" for bright young men, contributing ideas for inventions. He married Ivory's mother in 1921, and in the early 1920s they moved to Berkeley, where he commuted by ferryboat to San Francisco to a good position with the Weyerhaeuser Lumber company. Then in 1933, in partnership with an investor from Los Angeles who was in the lumber business and put up most of the money, he bought a mill in Klamath Falls, Oregon, and established the Ivory Pine Company. It was in Klamath Falls that Ivory spent his formative years.

Until the age of thirteen, Ivory was taught by nuns at a parochial school. "But I wouldn't say," Ivory remarks, "that I had a religious upbringing. I had a somewhat theatrically devout period in seventh grade, for a few months, but that is the only time I can remember." His boyhood imagination had a theatrical turn in other ways, for with his sister Charlotte, three years younger, and the neighboring children, he improvised a stage, using a simple platform, on which they took the roles of actors. Before long his father built them a proper "theater," with an unadorned, roll-up canvas curtain. "There wasn't much in the way of sets," Ivory recalls, "and we didn't do much in the way of plays, but it was a theater." Even as a boy, he was fascinated by buildings,

My father told me that when he worked for Edison there was a box with a slotted top attached to the boss's office door. Fledgling inventors were to drop into this any ideas they might have thought up. Edison would refine and then patent them if they were any good; the idea man did not expect to share in his invention financially. I remember my father's good-natured laugh when he recounted this. We had a group photo of the old inventor surrounded by all his bright young men—including my father—which Edison had signed and which I still have. Edison's name is somewhat smeared; I tested it as a child by spitting on my finger in order to see if the signature was really written in ink and not engraved. This was no doubt after seeing the movie *Edison, the Man,* starring Spencer Tracy. Though skeptical, I must have realized the value of a signed photograph by the inventor of the light bulb and the phonograph—not to mention sprocketed celluloid motion-picture film and the Kinetoscope, which Edison in time developed as the Vitascope, the first commercially successful motion-picture projector. JI

European and American, and by decor. "If you grew up in a raw Western town, as I did," he comments, "in a place that had no buildings, except very peculiar and flimsy ones, your eye is forever searching the landscape for something more solid."

Like others of his age, he also went to movies, and he admits to having been spellbound by *Gone with the Wind*. With its great earthquake scene, *San Francisco* fascinated him and he would later see it over and over: "I was always crazy about disaster movies: typhoons and tidal waves and shipwrecks." He says that in high school he "ate up Bette Davis movies." *Mr. Skeffington* was a favorite. Ivory's father sold lumber to Metro-Goldwyn-Mayer, and in 1943, when he was fourteen, Ivory was taken to the studio's sound stages. The experience helped to decide him on a career in films as a set designer.

At eighteen, Ivory was admitted to the University of Oregon in Eugene, where he studied architecture because of his liking for buildings and their interiors, but also to prepare himself for the sets he would one day design. But in his junior year he switched to a general fine-arts course and, as a result, took an extra year to graduate. In the summer of 1950, a year before he graduated, he traveled to Europe to visit Paris (with a side trip to Venice), with an idea of enrolling at the IDHEC, the Paris film school. But at that time the Korean War began, which would have meant being drafted unless he returned to college. So he returned to finish his degree and then enrolled in the graduate program in filmmaking at the University of Southern California—by which time he had ceased to think of himself as a set designer, or as that merely.

He found the film school at USC uninspiring, admits to having "hated" it. Instruction was largely in the making of industrial films, which sometimes demonstrated the use of industrial gadgets and labor-saving methods for the training of workers. His senior project, markedly more aesthetic, was a three-minute short called "Four in the Morning," based on a poem by Edith Sitwell set to William Walton's "Façade" music. "It was completely surrealist—or what I thought of then as surrealist—in its images," he told me. "It had shots, for instance, in which a sea urchin eats a playing card, things like that. I say 'surrealist.' I think it was more desperation on my part. It was the rhythmical chanting of words and music that was the impetus to do that film, and the sound track was more important to me probably than the images, so I went out and tried to create the images that would go with the sound track. The film still exists."

His MA thesis film, *Venice: Theme and Variations*, was inspired by his visit to Venice in 1950. "I wanted to do something on my own," he said. "I liked the city, it seemed a wonderful place to make a movie. But I didn't know much about the place of Venice in the grand scheme of things." His father, who was always supportive of his son in his choice of career, enabled him to do the film by advancing $15,000, quite a lot of money in 1952 for a half-hour documentary. In Venice, he shot a suitcaseful of 16mm film that was to depict "a history of the city in

My first movie job was as a production assistant on a 16mm film about how mail is delivered by helicopter to the Los Angeles suburbs. I couldn't work up much excitement. And when the school invited Hollywood veterans to talk to the students, I sat fidgeting, my eyes glazing over, as these distinguished men tried to interest us. William Cameron Menzies, the production designer of *Gone with the Wind*, ought to have made some impression on me, but he failed to. Now that I am myself on the receiving end, I've realized that it must always be like that with film students, who inevitably yawn and sprawl and size you up cynically. After I had become a director, I attended a class Jean Renoir was teaching at the UCLA film school. I don't know why I expected the hush of High Mass, but I did, as this immensely civilized, great, and patient old man gave the most delicate and precise instruction on building shots, while his audience shambled in and out, and ate yogurt. JI

(opposite) One of the peculiar buildings dotting the landscape of southern Oregon, and a very dizzy architectural conception it is: Egypt's Temple of Karnak with glass walls.

terms of its art.'' But when he returned to USC and conferred with his faculty adviser, Lester Novros, the conception was refocused as a chronicle not of historical events but of painters' changing views of Venice; and Ivory subsequently traveled to New York and Boston to film paintings of Venice in museums and private collections.

Before long, however, he *was* drafted, and for the next two years was an NCO in the U. S. Army's Special Services with the Second Armored Division in Germany, working as a producer's assistant on soldier shows. The assignment, which proved congenial, enabled him to travel in Europe, and to revisit Venice to shoot further footage for his film. After his discharge from the army, Ivory returned to USC and completed the editing of *Venice: Theme and Variations*—which was shown at the Edinburgh Festival in 1957 and later cited in *The New York Times* as one of the year's ten best documentaries.

At the Red Fort in Delhi, during the shooting of *The Delhi Way* in 1960, Ivory operates the camera, with his assistant, Toon Ghose, standing left.

While making *Venice,* Ivory had begun to school himself in eighteenth-century art, an interest that led him one day to the gallery of Raymond Lewis, a San Francisco print dealer. There, spread on a table, were a number of Indian miniature paintings that he found exciting. As yet he knew little of India or its art, but it seemed to him from his experience of making *Venice* that the Indian paintings could be photographed very strikingly. In the time ahead Ivory read all that he could find on Indian history and art, and—again financed by his father—searched out Indian miniatures on the West and East coasts, in both museums and private collections. The documentary that resulted, *The Sword and the Flute,* was quite justly acclaimed when it was shown in New York, and it began to attract attention to him.

After a screening of *The Sword and the Flute,* along with *Venice,* at a New York party, Paul Sherbert, then head of the Asia Society, asked Ivory if he would like to go to India to make a film about Delhi. He said that he would, and Sherbert then arranged sponsorship from Mrs. John D. Rockefeller III, one of the Asia Society's patrons, who provided a $20,000 commission for two documentaries, on Delhi and Afghanistan. Although he shot several thousand feet of 16mm film in and around Kabul, the Afghanistan film was never completed; but *The Delhi Way* was, although not until after he had made his first feature film, *The Householder.* Ivory shot scenes in Delhi from January to October 1960, with the side trip to Kabul; by then, his grant having been used up, he returned to New York, longing to return to India, with which he had now fallen in love, to complete his film. Early in 1961, he met Merchant, and by the end of the year Merchant Ivory Productions came into being.

Three decades later, the once-fledgling maker of 16mm documentaries has achieved renown as the director of many feature films, but in certain respects they have grown out of his earliest efforts—in their international settings and interest in the captured moment of the life of a culture. The extraordinary visual sense of the early documentaries has led to movies noted for the beauty and expert composition of their imagery. Ivory makes pictures that have atmosphere and resonance and has never made a movie, irrespective of results, that has not possessed a sense of style. It is often said that Ivory's films have his personal stamp on them—a way of speaking, perhaps, of personal qualities that enter into them: sophistication, tolerant affection, sharp wit, a feeling for place. A rapt interest in buildings has also been a feature of Ivory's filmmaking. His buildings all have stories to tell—the Mission Inn in *The Wild Party,* the Beechwood mansion in *Savages,* the Taj Mahal Hotel in *Bombay Talkie,* the family house in *Mr. and Mrs. Bridge.* The fiber embedded in old structures becomes part of the poetic language of his films. Ivory also has an attraction in his films to obliqueness, because obliqueness may leave deep reverberations—thus all the nuance in his movies, the unstated things, the shaded meanings. Reviewers sometimes grouse that he is *too* oblique and that the pacing of his movies is too slow, but his way is to be careful and probing as he creates

(opposite) Blythe Danner, in *Mr. and Mrs. Bridge.*

(below) Paul Newman and Robert Sean Leonard, in *Mr. and Mrs. Bridge.*

texture and verisimilitude. He can't be hurried. "You have to incur his art," film critic Andrew Sarris told me, "layer by layer; it doesn't come rushing out at you."

Ivory has the reputation of being a perfectionist, which may be, but he is also an instinctive director. The late Anne Baxter once compared the directing styles of Alfred Hitchcock and Ivory, under both of whom she had worked. "Hitch," she remarked, "had seen the film totally finished in his head before shooting, so it was almost boring for him to put it on film. Hitch wasn't always nice. It was difficult if you felt strongly about something he hadn't planned on. But Jim gets inspired right on the spot; he would like to shoot the whole thing like an improvisation. He doesn't sit you down and intellectualize the scene at all. He depends a lot on intuition, and he wants the unexpected."

In my interview with him in New York, Christopher Reeve gave a good account of what it is like to act under Ivory's direction. "What Jim does beautifully," he said, "is to collect people around him who are passionate in their work, and to use the best of what they can do, whether it is the cameraman, the actors, the costume designers. He absorbs it all, and when he's got all their input, he just stands back and uses the best of it. The actors need somebody with a rational and dispassionate intelligence to say, 'Thank you so much for all these things you're bringing me, now here are the ones I want to use.' He's a terrific judge of what's good and what isn't. Sometimes he doesn't know exactly how something should be done better, or what's wrong with it. But he certainly can say, 'No, not that. Let's try something else.' You end up really wanting to please."

Ivory also tends to remain close to actors (and production people) with whom he has worked. It is remarkable that in making his second feature film, *Shakespeare Wallah*, he should have cast Shashi Kapoor, Madhur Jaffrey, Utpal Dutt, and Jennifer and Felicity Kendal—all of whom were just starting out but were to go on to have significant careers. Thereafter, together with Saeed Jaffrey (who had been the narrator for both Merchant and Ivory's first films), they were to appear in many of Ivory's Indian films in a variety of roles, rather like the actors who regularly appear in the movies of Ingmar Bergman.

As the settings of his films moved beyond India, Ivory continued to discover new talent. Prominent performers—Maggie Smith, James Mason, Alan Bates, Julie Christie, Peggy Ashcroft, Vanessa Redgrave, Isabel Adjani, Paul Newman, and Joanne Woodward among others—have appeared in his films; but he has shown a special talent for identifying and using actors before they became well known. He cast Christopher Walken in his first featured role, Sam Waterston before he became successful in Hollywood, and Rupert Graves and James Wilby when they were literally unknown. But he has been particularly uncanny in discovering young actresses—Felicity Kendal, Sean Young, Greta Scacchi, Madeleine Potter, and Helena Bonham Carter for instance—at the outset of their careers. He also likes to use supporting actors in more than one film, sometimes with witty variations in the parts they play. A "lofty-minded" clergyman in *A Room with a View*, Patrick Godfrey becomes a dirty-minded servant in *Maurice*; a sturdy New England patriarch of scrupulous probity in *The Europeans*, Wesley Addy next appears as a mesmerist-humbug in *The Bostonians*. Ivory's loyalty to his actors is reciprocated: a place in the Merchant Ivory family is coveted.

Ivory is not only a director but a director-writer, who wrote intelligent scripts for his early documentaries, has co-written a number of his feature films, and has been influential in the screenplays produced by Jhabvala. He has also written introductions to books and contributed articles to magazines and journals. He has written many unsigned "Talk of the Town" pieces (one on the arrival in New York of Satyajit Ray) for *The New Yorker*, and he has been the author of signed ones for *Sight and Sound* and other journals—about his own films and about the films of other directors. In all of these articles, he writes with grace and naturalness, and with very pleasing effect. When Ivory is not directing or writing, he enjoys reading. The closets of his upstate house, Cyrus Jhabvala told me, are "all stuffed with books," which are read and circulated among Ivory and his friends.

The differences in personality between Merchant and Ivory are striking and have often been pointed out by journalists, who like to depict them as the brash Indian and the reserved American, or to carry the contrast further, to see them as a reconstituted version of Anglo India. The contrast serves well enough as a convenient shorthand for their differences, but it is not at all exact. Merchant isn't merely "brash"; he is also shrewd, practical, and managing. And Ivory isn't merely reserved; he knows exactly what he wants and how to get his way. On a social level, Merchant clearly is more gregarious and outgoing, while Ivory can seem shy or withdrawn; yet he has—and it is one of the things about him that strikes me most—an unusual gift for intimacy. This quality of intimacy is in his films, in the articles he writes (with their beguiling blend of urbanity and unassumingness), and in his conversation, which can be delightful. "Jim doesn't always feel the need to make conversation," Madhur Jaffrey remarks, "but when he gets going, when he wants to talk, he's absolutely wonderful to talk to." He has a comically dry wit, is possessed of a receptive and playful mind, and is forever conceiving new film projects he wants to do.

Ivory is a greatly attracting man who has brought all manner of people (Merchant and Jhabvala included) into his orbit. What has held the partners together for so long appears to involve more than their need to merge their talents. Loyalty is important to all three. Madhur Jaffrey speaks of the "deep emotional bond" that exists among them. Their partnership has not only endured but also made the *Guinness Book of World Records* as the longest collaboration in film history. The collaboration of a European, an Indian, and an American would have been hard to predict, but the success of their enterprise might not have been foreseen either. They are full of surprises, these three unique and uncommon individuals who make unique and uncommon films.

CHAPTER II

The Late Fifties—Mid-Sixties
—Beginnings

VENICE: THEME AND VARIATIONS
(1957)

IVORY'S INITIAL EFFORT as a filmmaker was *Venice: Theme and Variations*, a documentary made as his master's thesis at the USC film school that, although only 28 minutes long, is rich in composition and aesthetic texture. Picturesque buildings along the canals are mirrored in the undulating reflection of water below them; a figure in darkened bronze atop a bell tower strikes a huge bell with a long-handled hammer, tolling the hour; boatmen are observed on the lagoons in the bluish haze of dusk. These glimpses of present-day Venice alternate with passages in which the paintings Ivory has photographed vividly, accompanied by mood-setting music—from Gabrieli, Vivaldi, Monteverdi, and Chopin—present artists' views of Venice over centuries of time.

Early sequences consist of Gentile Bellini's depictions of early clerics firm in their faith; and of scenes from Carpaccio, of a lighter narrative line, which draw attention to the daily life being lived in the palazzos and squares of the old city. The changing milieu of Venice is then traced from the sixteenth century, when the city was an important center of wealth and trade, to the eighteenth, portrayed by Guardi and Longhi, when Venice had entered into an irrevocable decline. Ivory

(above left) The Piazzetta, Venice, photographed by Ivory in 1952. Forty years on, the scene now resembles shots in his later costume films like *A Room with a View.*

(above right) An early 18th-century drawing by Francesco Guardi, which appears in *Venice: Theme and Variations.*
Piazzetta, Looking Toward San Giorgio Maggiore; Pen and brown ink, brown wash, 6 × 10¼"; The Metropolitan Museum of Art, Rogers Fund, 1937 (37.165.78)

admits that it was the eighteenth century "that interested me most, Guardi and Longhi"; and it is a period certainly that offers an unusually rich sense of Venetian society, with its world of the theater, of carnival, and other diversions that give it a strong sense of atmosphere, place, and moment.

A problem Ivory faced in making the film is that no documentary so brief could possibly treat fully artists' visions of Venice. The result, as he himself has pointed out, is that one is likely to have a sense of gaps and omissions. The High Renaissance of Titian, Tintoretto, and Veronese is missing. And after the eighteenth century, the film leaps forward to Whistler at the end of the nineteenth, whose impressionistic

(opposite above) *The Arrival of the Ambassadors*, from *The Legend of St. Ursula*, the late 15th-century series by the Venetian painter Vittorio Carpaccio. Gallerie dell'Accademia

(opposite below) Another kind of ambassador, this one from America: a Mr. Bridge–like figure and his gondolier, drawn by Saul Steinberg, c. 1955. Courtesy the artist.

(above) Ivory during filming in the San Diego Art Museum; the painting is by the Venetian artist Pietro Longhi.

landscapes offer little direct commentary on the social life of the city; and then as suddenly it leaps to the drawings of Saul Steinberg in the mid-twentieth century. The light and delightful Steinberg, however, is a good note on which to end. Instead of being lit by melancholy moonlight, his bustling Venice is brightened by neon, accompanied by cabaret noises and the rhythms of a tango. The Piazza San Marco becomes an immense café with orchestras and the comic figures of waiters sketched in with a few lines. Silly, cube-shaped birds perch on the arches of buildings, and satiric gondolas ply the canals. One of the gondolas in close-up resembles a spaceship, from the panel window of which an American tourist couple stare sternly and blankly. A documentary on Venice might easily have been too earnest, too heavy. Steinberg's whimsical drawings at the end, however, reveal how Ivory has brought to the film something of his own wry sense of humor, making it "personal" as well as formal.

THE SWORD AND THE FLUTE
(1959)

IVORY'S SECOND DOCUMENTARY, *The Sword and the Flute*, also dealing with schools of art, grew out of his experience in making *Venice*. Only here, instead of photographing works by the Italian masters, he has used superb specimens of Indian miniature paintings. Ivory's intelligent script, narrated with feeling by Saeed Jaffrey, and accompanied by the music of Ravi Shankar and Ali Akbar Khan, traces the history of Indian miniature painting after the Moghul invasion as it develops into two principal schools, the Moghul (Muslim) and the Rajput (Hindu). The Moghul miniatures reflect an interest in historical events and the life of the court, while those of the Rajput emphasize otherworldly concerns, the yearning for transcendence, but both involve the viewer immediately in a world that is exotic and ravishing. Ivory is fascinated by the faces (and prominent eyes) of his figures, the garments they wear, and the sharply noted details of their surroundings; the figures seem almost to leap at the viewer. Compared to *Venice*, the dramas Ivory creates through the Indian scenes are tauter and give a greater sense of complexity, which comes in part from the tension in Ivory between his intellectual role as a close observer of culture and his intimate, empathetic response to the paintings' exceptional sensuousness and romantic feeling. The cameraman for the film was another USC cinema student, Mindaugis Bagdon, and his and Ivory's photography of the Indian miniatures proved so effective that Ivory would use the technique later, also with striking effect, in his film *Hullabaloo Over Georgie and Bonnie's Pictures*.

As I pointed out somewhere else, Indian miniature painting is the subject matter, but the film is really a sort of dream of India as imagined by someone who has never been there and only knows the country through its art and music. JI

38

(opposite) *Bhairvi Rag* (left) and *Asavari Ragini* (right), early 18th-century Indian miniatures painted at Delhi. The first Indian miniatures Ivory acquired, they helped to inspire *The Sword and the Flute*.

(right) Merchant and the dancer Jane Mosley appear as human puppets in a short 16mm film that was a warm-up for his *Creation of Woman*, c. 1960.

THE CREATION OF WOMAN
(1960)

A YEAR AFTER *The Sword and the Flute*, Merchant produced his first film, the 14-minute short *The Creation of Woman*. Made while he was working at the McCann-Erickson advertising agency, it was shot on the most meager of budgets, a mere $9,000 advanced by Charles Schwep, an acquaintance of the time, partner in the endeavor, and the film's director. At first Merchant considered starring in the film, but Schwep wanted a seasoned professional, and in something of a coup they engaged the celebrated Indian dancer Bhaskar Roy Chaudhuri for the leading role. *The Creation of Woman* begins with the story of the Hindu god Brahma, whose role as creator also encompasses the Christian account of Adam and Eve. The brief film is essentially an anecdote. After Adam calls on God to give him a female partner, Eve is created and Adam finds that he can neither live with nor without her. Photographed in bold colors (with costumes of red and gold set against a dazzling blue backdrop), Merchant's parable is set to music and dance, with Chaudhuri performing his splendidly sensual and athletic Dance of Shiva that in pantomime tells the story of man's beginnings. An arresting tour de force, the film seems relevant to Merchant himself, who selects the creation story for his theme as he creates himself as a filmmaker.

THE HOUSEHOLDER
(1963)

I T WAS NOT LONG after the release of *The Creation of Woman* that Merchant and Ivory first met and agreed to form an Indo-American film production company. Merchant left New York in May 1961, and in November of that year Ivory joined him in India hoping to undertake their first venture together, a movie called *Devgar* that the anthropologist Gitel Steed had written about life in a Gujerati village. Merchant was to be its producer, Sidney Meyers its director, and Ivory its photographer. But the project failed to materialize when funding could not be obtained, and Merchant and Ivory turned to another project, the filming of Jhabvala's novel *The Householder*. Although she had no previous experience as a scriptwriter, Jhabvala soon produced a screenplay without too much difficulty. But something at least was salvaged from the unrealized Gujerati film, since two actors who were to have appeared in it became the stars of *The Householder*—Shashi Kapoor, then at the beginning of his enormously successful film career, and Leela Naidu, a young French-Indian actress who had been in two previous Indian films. Importantly, Ivory also obtained the services of Satyajit Ray's cameraman Subrata Mitra, who kept him, he says, from making many of the beginner's common mistakes.

Initial investment in the film came from Ivory's father and from private sources in Bombay, but midway in the shooting the money ran out. Merchant approached other potential backers in Bombay, but they

(above left) Indu (Leela Naidu) confides in her sympathetic landlady, played by Achla Sachdev.

(above right) Prem (Shashi Kapoor), with his domineering mother (Durga Khote).

(opposite) Prem is told by a swami (Pahari Sanyal, *far right*) that, as a householder with much work to do in the world, he must not think of quitting it too prematurely.

did not regard *The Householder* as a commercially promising venture, and the partners were also turned down by India's Film Financing Corporation. "We were introduced," Merchant remembers, "to a money-lender. We wanted $25,000. He said he would give us $20,000 and deduct $5,000 as interest first. We were devastated." Finally, however, a Bombay cinema owner who had been one of the original investors came through with additional money, and with further financial help from Ivory's father, they were able to finish the film, which was made, respectively, in English and Hindi language versions, and in all cost $125,000.

Satyajit Ray also played a role in the completion of the film. Ivory had first seen Ray's *Pather Panchali* (1955) while working on *The Sword and the Flute* in San Francisco. "I had never seen a film," he observed, "that so thrilled me. It was not just the story—poor struggling Indians in a village in Bengal—it was the presentation: the

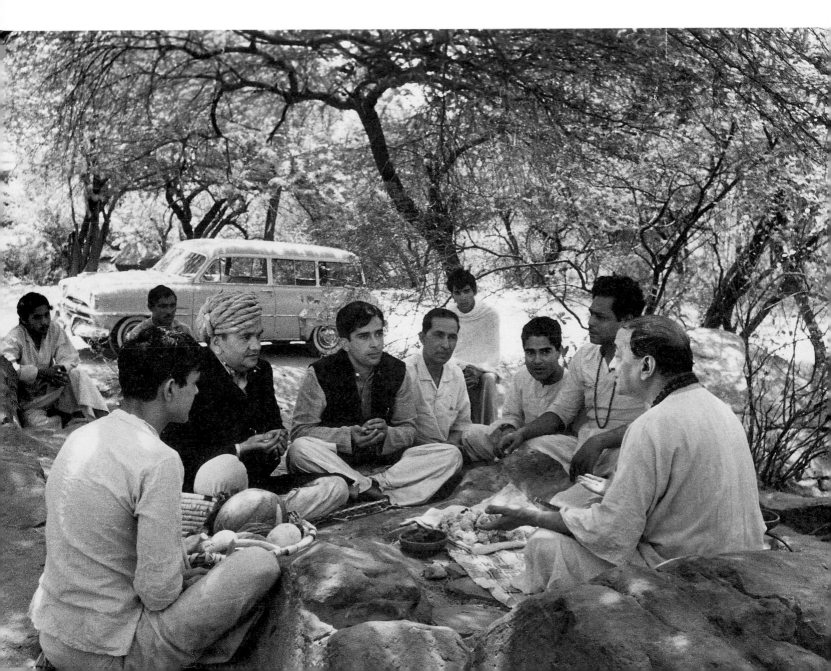

beauty of the images, the intoxicating sounds, the music, the lyricism of it." While in India early in 1961, Ivory sought out Ray and came to be on fairly friendly terms with him, and after shooting *The House-holder* he consulted him about the film. Ray contributed to it in part by supervising what music went into it and how it was recorded. In addition, when Ivory asked him how the film could be improved by further editing, Ray offered to recut it for them to give it a tighter structure. He recut the entire film in only three days, importantly creating the device of the encompassing flashback. "I stood by and watched," Ivory remarked, "and in a way the experience of seeing how he recut the film has been the basis of our work in the editing room ever since then. We always cut the film according to the script, and then afterward there is a tremendous upheaval in the cutting room. We throw things out and change things. If I had not seen the way Ray could reorganize material, so skillfully and easily, I probably would have remained more cautious about big changes." But Ray also seems

The wedding procession that closes *The Householder.*

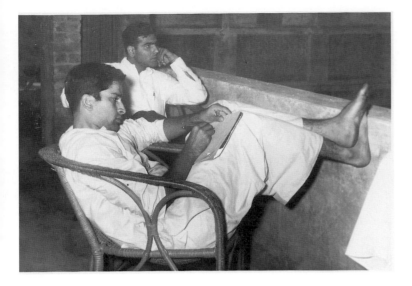

(above left) Shashi Kapoor and his producer, relaxing on the set of *The Householder*. Both are about twenty-five years old. (1962)

(above right) Ruth Jhabvala with her daughters and James Ivory at Juhu Beach near Bombay in the summer of 1962; (left to right) Renana, Ava, and Firoza.

(below) Subrata Mitra, Merchant and Ivory's first cameraman (He was also Satyajit Ray's). (1962)

influential on *The Householder* in other ways. His poetic realism and his ability to endow simple characters and their lives, which contain no really big events, with drama, shapes Ivory's approach to the movie.

Jhabvala's novel concerns the coming of age of an ingenuous Indian youth named Prem. Previously sheltered by his family, he assumes the responsibilities of husband and provider in a marriage not of his choosing but arranged by his widowed orthodox Hindu mother and elder relatives. As a language teacher at a third-rate college, he can hardly support himself, and he finds the adjustment of living with his new wife awkward. One of the humorous strategies of the novel is that Prem should constantly search for guidance from his elders, whose examples of blunted sensibility or resignation close all avenues to expansion. In adapting her novel to the screen, Jhabvala makes Prem's situation somewhat more positive. In the novel his dawning attraction to his wife enables him to bear what might be called his doom; but in the film his adjustment to lowered expectations is less painful, since his eventual happiness with his wife is brought out more fully. At the conclusion, he even counsels a dejected bridegroom, a little pompously, on the pleasures of the married state.

Prem and his wife are essentially children, unacquainted with the realities of the world. But the other characters have the limited horizons of children in their self-centeredness. Mr. Khanna, the principal of the school, played with fine deadpan self-satisfaction by Romesh Thappar, speaks of responsibility while taking advantage of his teachers, paying them the most minimal wages. Mr. Chadda, the history teacher, finds an illusion of importance through his pomposity and by tyrannizing the younger teachers. Prem's landlord Mr. Saigal (Pincho Kapoor) is heavy-set and indolent, oblivious to all but his creature comforts of cards and bootlegged liquor. Prem's mother, played wonderfully by Durga Khote, is also deeply self-centered, dabbing ostentatiously at her eyes with the hem of her sari as she imagines that her children have

(left) A "star-studded" premiere for *The Householder*, given by American Ambassador John Kenneth Galbraith (*far left*) at his residence in New Delhi. Prime Minister Nehru is flanked by Ruth Jhabvala and Ismail Merchant. Also present was Indira Gandhi, who kept a wary eye on her father—he had been unwell—from a third-row banquette she shared with director Ivory. (1963)

(*opposite*) Freshly dyed turbans drying in front of the Jammi Masjid in Old Delhi, an important sequence from *The Delhi Way*. The turbans most often seen were in shades of brilliant pink, canary yellow, and lime green.

neglected her. These characters are all types, bordering on caricature, but it is surprising how well they play. Many of the characters come together satirically at a tea party at the school in which the men are arranged awkwardly at one side of the room while the women are segregated at the other—the first of the ghastly and failed social occasions to be seen in many Merchant Ivory films.

Ivory is less successful with the characters who have come to India from abroad. Ernest, a young American from Philadelphia who comes to India in search of spiritual values, is played by Ernest Castaldo too broadly to be believable. The other Westerners with whom he shares a house—a middle-aged woman who has become a convert to yoga, and an old Englishman who does gardening while Beethoven blares from a phonograph—are never really developed. The film is on surer ground, in a manner reminiscent of Ray, in its gentle, ironic exploration of the evolving relationship of Prem and Indu, to whom Kapoor and Naidu give freshness and charm. The camera work of Mitra, working for the first time outside Bengal and for a director other than Ray, is consistently sensitive to the Indian settings and landscapes; and Ivory has a sharp eye for details, for little captured moments. In a flashback, Indu sees herself again as a young girl in a swing in a country setting; in his loneliness Prem is framed by a window as he stares pensively and somberly before him; Prem and Ernest walk together along a broad road strewn with autumn leaves while misty light shines luminously through the boughs of trees. Quiet moments of visual perception, the images complement the observant spirit of the film that, although modest and sometimes awkward, seems full of promise.

For me, the reward of *The Householder* was that it was distributed by a major Hollywood studio, Columbia Pictures. For a first feature, the prestige was great. *The Householder*, unfortunately, was not a success at the box office, but it was seen and written about favorably by critics and journalists.

It also led to a friendship with Vivian Leigh, whom we invited to a screening of *The Householder* at Columbia's Fifth Avenue screening room. Kay Brown— the legendary agent who put David Selznick together with the unpublished manuscript of *Gone with the Wind*—for some reason acceded to our request to meet Miss Leigh. We were totally unknown, but she came to the screening. Jim and I sat on either side of her, cheekily hoping to enlist her for a project of our own. We wanted her to play the formidable Lady Sale, wife of the British general who led the ill-fated retreat from Kabul in 1842. She liked *The Householder* and agreed to let us take her to dinner at Top of the Sixes across the street.

Two years later, Miss Leigh visited India, where she had lived as a child, and to which she had never returned. I'd read in the Indian newspapers that, in answer to a reporter's questions about Indian films, she had praised *The Householder* and was looking forward to working with us. I met her at the Bombay airport with the traditional garland.

We planned for her first day an outing to the Elephanta Caves, which are on an island off Bombay. We filled a hamper with all sorts of delicacies, including a thermos of gimlets, and hired a boat. But when I called her from the lobby of the Taj Mahal Hotel to tell her to come down, she said she couldn't—she felt rotten, hadn't slept, and must give up Elephanta. Jim said, "Let's go anyway," as he'd never been there, so we went; he devoured all the

THE DELHI WAY
(1964)

delicacies and all the gimlets, but I was heavy-hearted. What if she didn't turn up for the party I was throwing for her that night, to which the biggest Bombay film stars and socialites were coming?

When we got back, I went straight to the Taj Mahal, where we ran into her in the lobby. She was in a chirpy mood and wanted to see a cricket match, to shop in Crawford Market, to have iced drinks at street stalls, etc. We reminded her of the party, and she replied, "Yes, darling, hmmm, hmmm . . ."

The party was at the mansion of a friend, Sunita Pitamber, and everybody seemed to turn out for it. The stars seemed to arrive in the order of their importance: small-fry first, then bigger and bigger. With each entry, a ritual was enacted: the doorbell would ring, all heads would turn. As the night wore on and we chattered ever more desperately and bravely, ever more grandly dressed Indian stars would arrive to be met by ever more disappointed looks. But in the end she didn't fail us. The last person to arrive, she was introduced to each guest and flashed them the same sparkling-eyed smile that Scarlett O'Hara had at the ball in *Gone with the Wind*. We would meet her again but regretfully never work with her. IM

THE DELHI WAY—produced, written, photographed, and directed by Ivory—was begun before *The Householder* but completed after it. A documentary of Delhi, it scans the city's historic past that includes successive Afghan, Moghul, and English invasions, while it reveals its variegated life of the present. At the opening a train moves along a landscape in darkness to evoke (as in a film by Ray) the passage of time; and past and present are thereafter anchored in contrasting views of Shah Jahan's Red Fort and King George V's new city. The film, in which time has a devouring quality, is impressionistic as it takes in the new city. An army of civil servants in white garments ride to work on bicycles, while an anonymous beggar sits nodding by a roadside tree; an upper-middle-class flower show on the grounds of a private club appears side-by-side with views of dust storms, constricted slum dwellings, crowded bazaars, and posters of Indian film idols. Ivory evokes the bewildering legacy of Delhi, and if the film finally lacks the intense sense of involvement of *The Sword and the Flute*, it does act as an effective bridge to *Shakespeare Wallah*, in which time and change are central concerns.

45

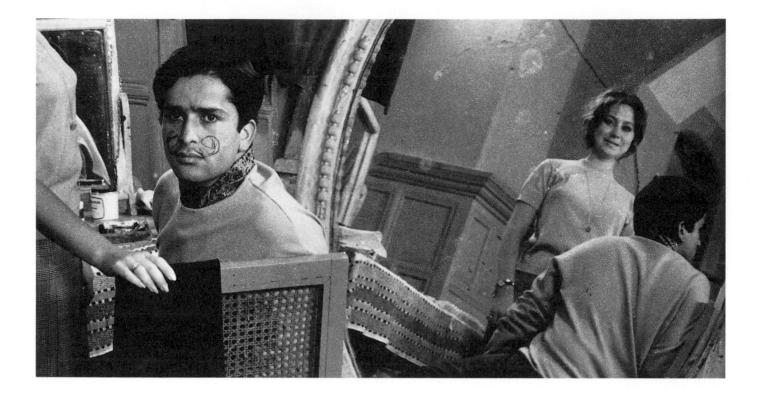

SHAKESPEARE WALLAH
(1965)

SHAKESPEARE WALLAH came about when Geoffrey Kendal, actor-manager of a troupe of touring English players in India called Shakespeariana, let Ivory see the diary he kept of his company's experiences in 1947, when India achieved independence. When Ivory showed it to Jhabvala, she became excited, sensing that the diary account could be developed into a film so as to become a metaphor for the end of the British Raj. Kendal and his wife, Laura Liddel, were enlisted to play their counterparts, renamed the Buckinghams; their daughters Jennifer and Felicity were also to have roles in the picture, Felicity as the romantic lead opposite Shashi Kapoor, Jennifer's real-life husband. None of the events in the film, however, draws directly on the experience of the Kendals, and in important respects *Shakespeare Wallah* runs counter to Kendal's sense of the success his troupe enjoyed in India. As Kendal records in his autobiography, *The Shakespeare Wallah* (1986), it took him years to be reconciled to a movie about the failure of a theatrical company in India, in many ways uncomfortably resembling his own.

Shakespeare Wallah was made on a shoestring budget of $80,000, obtained chiefly from the sale of the world distribution rights of *The Householder* to Columbia Pictures. The film was made in black-and-white because Merchant and Ivory did not have the money to shoot it in color. Unable to afford studio sets, they shot everything on

The rights to *The Householder*, which we sold to Columbia Pictures, were paid for out of their frozen, or "blocked," rupee account in India. All the American distribution companies had over the years piled up enormous amounts of money from the distribution in India of their always-popular films. But only a small amount of that money could be repatriated, due to the stringent foreign-exchange regulations of the Indian government. The money could, however, be used for film production in India and, after much persuasion by me, for the outright purchase of Indian films like *The Householder*. We used the money from Columbia to make *Shakespeare Wallah*, and later on, 20th Century Fox spent a lot of *its* frozen rupees on *The Guru*. These kinds of arrangements were the real financial underpinnings of our company in its early years. IM

(above left) Backstage at the Gaiety Theater in Simla. Sanju (Shashi Kapoor) and Lizzie Buckingham (Felicity Kendal), in a scene from *Shakespeare Wallah*.

(above right) The film star Manjula (Madhur Jaffrey) during a moment from her song and dance number in the film within a film in *Shakespeare Wallah*.

46

It wasn't that we really couldn't afford to shoot in a studio—probably we could have found the money. But I preferred (and still do) real locations: real houses, streets, offices, theaters, churches, and of course, palaces of every kind. They inspire me more than studio creations can, despite the fact that many of my favorite films (including Satyajit Ray's) are studio films. The real has texture and atmosphere and the solidity of monuments. Remember the scene at the end of *Gone with the Wind*, in which Scarlett comes running out of Ashley Wilkes's house in search of Rhett? The porch column she grabs shakes in her hand. I saw this when I was eleven and it made a strong impression. JI

location—in the hill station of Kasauli, in the Punjab; in the Vice-Regal summer capital of Simla; in Alwar, in Rajasthan; in Lucknow; and in Bombay. When the film was cut, Ivory took it to Calcutta to show to Satyajit Ray, asking if he would consent to write the musical score; the score he provided, recorded in a Calcutta studio in two long sessions, enhances the film markedly. It was entered in competition at the 1965 Berlin Film Festival, where Madhur Jaffrey won a Silver Bear award for Best Actress, and in the fall was shown at the New York Film Festival, where it received highly favorable reviews. American distributors, however, were wary of taking it on, believing that an Indian film without famous stars had poor commercial prospects. Merchant Ivory bore the expense of opening the film themselves at Walter Reade's Baronet Theatre in New York with an understanding that Walter Reade-Sterling would distribute it if it did well. After a strong opening-day showing, and a favorable review in *The New York Times*, the Reade organization accepted it for distribution. *Shakespeare Wallah* found a relatively modest audience at first but in time attracted a much larger one as it came to be recognized as a classic.

Its story is quite simple. Against the background of the passing of British culture in post-independence India, a young girl, Lizzie Buckingham (Felicity Kendal), a member of her parents' roving troupe of Shakespearean actors, meets and falls in love with Sanju (Shashi Kapoor), a wealthy young Indian playboy. Their romance blossoms but is subjected to a variety of conflicts, and in the end the lovers separate; Lizzie is sent off to England by her parents who recognize that there is no future for her (and very little for them) in the new India. The art of the film depends very much on skillful handling, provided partly by Jhabvala and Ivory's tactful and finely modulated screenplay, and by the consistently appealing performances of its actors. Felicity Kendal, eighteen at the time, plays Lizzie with a remarkable freshness and naturalness that are matched by Kapoor's assured playing of Sanju. They are strongly supported by Utpal Dutt, on his way to becoming one of India's finest actors, as the Maharaja who hosts the Buckinghams' performance of *Anthony and Cleopatra* in his palace, half of which, in changed times, has been rented out as office space; and Madhur Jaffrey as Manjula, the beautiful and flashingly temperamental Indian film actress who has prior claims on Sanju. The Kendals themselves, who had never previously appeared in a film, lend an air of reality to the picture, both in the scenes in which they perform on stage and in those in which they are behind-the-scenes strolling actors.

English reviews of *Shakespeare Wallah* frequently noted the influence on Ivory of Satyajit Ray, especially in his appreciation of the characters' humanity and of the physical textures of India. Much of the interest of *Shakespeare Wallah,* indeed, is its immersion in mood and atmosphere, the dreamlike setting that frames the declining fortunes of the old order and of the English colonials. This atmosphere, moreover, is complemented by the film's theatrical theme, by the players whose reality is make-believe but who must now, as the Maharaja concedes early in the movie, "make adjustments, come to terms with reality."

Ivory believes that making documentaries prepared him for *Shakespeare Wallah.* That background trained his eye for significant and telling detail but is also relevant in other ways. "The purpose of a documentary," he told an interviewer, "is to capture the experience, the essence of a subject." In *Shakespeare Wallah* he observes the experience of the Buckinghams from many sides, sensitive both to the humorous aspects and the melancholy of their situation; he is closely involved with them so that one responds to them with a feeling of intimacy, yet is distanced from them, too, and able to see them, as a documentary filmmaker might, from without.

Another feature of the film that can hardly be missed is Ivory's love of aesthetic textures and of striking imagery. If by default *Shakespeare Wallah* was shot in black-and-white, in many ways it merely enhances the film, enabling Ivory to work with evocative chiaroscuro effects. At the beginning, after the performance of Sheridan's *The Critic* on the grounds of an Indian college, the camera cuts to the compartment of a train that contains members of the Buckingham troupe, including Buckingham himself. The cut creates an ironic movement from the fixed and solid eighteenth-century past to a scene of flux, a world of time and change. Moreover, Buckingham is seen as a dark figure against the whitish light that floods in through the train window, an effect that heightens the sense of his own inner tension and the ambiguity that surrounds him.

The tension of ambiguity (partly in the conflict of cultures) in the light-versus-dark imagery appears throughout the picture, particularly

La Martinière, Lucknow, the setting for the opening sequence of *Shakespeare Wallah.* The enormous house—really a French palace set down with its formal parterres and Versailles–like artificial lake amidst mango groves on the vast Indian plain—was the creation of a French soldier of fortune, Claude Martin, who commanded the armies of the King of Oudh in about 1800.

in scenes involving Lizzie and Sanju. When the Buckinghams stay
overnight in the countryside, for example, Lizzie lies in bed inside
a tent, before the white gauze entrance of which one sees the dark sil-
houette of Sanju as he stands pensively smoking a cigarette. Light contrasted with dark imagery figures prominently again in the love scene
where they go walking in the woods. When they kiss, they are envel-
oped by a milky mist, and for a moment they seem to disappear, then
are visible again as dark figures in the mist. The tensions of their relationship, with its illusion and reality, are evoked, as it were, magically.

The theater life of the Buckinghams is a world of its own that
divides the lovers. When Sanju attempts to enter it in pursuit of Lizzie,
he incites Manjula's jealousy, and confusion results. At the same time,
the Buckinghams are restricted by their stage existence, cannot move
outward into the ongoing life of India. One is always conscious of them
as being constrained by their theatrical calling, which has lost popu-
larity to Indian films that represent the new, indigenous Indian culture.
The lovers, and the different spheres of life to which they belong,
become the metaphor of a changed world, the poignancy of which is
felt not just in them but also in the older people who give the idea, as
one critic called it, of "a middle-aged tragedy."

Arresting imagery of mourning can be noticed particularly in the
film. When the Buckinghams arrive at Glen Eagles, the resort that
once catered to them but is now being forced to close for lack of business, they come by rickshaw, in raincoats and umbrellas, like homeless
refugees. In a marvelous sequence at a moldy English club now belonging to its new Indian members, the old actor Bobby has Lizzie join him
in a waltz on a spacious dance floor where windows let in spotlighted
pools of light (like stage lighting)—until his heart begins to pain him

(above left) Carla Buckingham (Laura
Lidell) as Gertrude in *Hamlet*, with
Felicity Kendal as Ophelia; *(above right)*
Tony Buckingham (Geoffrey Kendal),
the manager-actor of the troupe of
Shakespearean players, as he removes his
grease paint after a disrupted perfor-
mance of *Othello*.

(opposite) Still at La Martinière: the
opening credit shot of *Shakespeare
Wallah*.

and they are forced to stop. Age and youth, the sense of the passage of time, are evoked affectingly. One notices, too, the sequence of shots that begin with Lizzie and Sanju in a car as they pass down the terraced highway of a steep hillside, Sanju singing blithefully. The camera cuts to the Buckinghams' old touring car that has to stop on the road as Bobby suffers a final heart attack. Ivory cuts to his funeral, and then to a close-up of Feste's clownish face in *Twelfth Night*, which has an almost mocking effect. Poetic and visually alive, *Shakespeare Wallah* is an extraordinary film. It is the jewel of Merchant Ivory's beginnings, hardly less than a miracle.

Ivory with Felicity Kendal at La Martinière. She is dressed for her role in Sheridan's *The Critic,* which in the film is performed for the boys college that inhabits the place today.

CHAPTER III

The Late Sixties—Early Seventies
—From India to America

THE GURU
(1969)

AFTER *SHAKESPEARE WALLAH*, Merchant Ivory became interested in two movie projects that in the end failed to materialize. One was a sequel to *Shakespeare Wallah* called *A Lovely World*, which followed the fortunes of Lizzie Buckingham in trendy London of the 1960s. Filmways commissioned Jhabvala to do the screenplay but when it was completed turned it down and the project was shelved. The other was to be a screen version of the novel *Vertical*

The Guru seems now to be a brightly colored fairy tale, a kind of 1960s fable, in which a muddled young urchin prince is deposited, via Air India's flying carpet, in a land of broad rivers, oriental domes, and harems full of plotting ladies. In this ever-so-puzzling kingdom, ruled over by an insecure despot who can thunder one moment and summon up divine music the next, our urchin prince has many strange adventures. There are witches who cast evil spells, magic amulets, a courtesan who is strangled by her own strings of pearls, cups containing mind-altering brews, and ancient seers who deal out both encouragement and fierce rebuke.

At the end of all his trials, the young prince, now enlightened, boards his magic carpet to return to his own far-off land. He is sheltering his treasure in his arms—the simple, good-hearted maiden he has set free from her imprisoning dreams, and who loves him. *The Guru*, the most unseen and mysterious of our movies, was Merchant Ivory's version of a sixties trip. To me anyway, it holds up as well—though some might say no better than—any of the others of the genre that have survived. JI

(opposite) A long-shut-up courtyard of the palace at Bikaner, one of the principal locations of *The Guru*. The Maharaja's sequestered ladies, locked in the purdah wing here, could watch events below through the pierced marble screens called *jalis*.

(below left to right) Michael York, Ivory, Rita Tushingham, and Utpal Dutt on location in Bombay. (1968)

and Horizontal (1963) by Lillian Ross, the well-known profile writer for *The New Yorker*. A comedy about upper-middle-class Jewish life in New York, the novel features an incompetent psychiatrist named Dr. Blauberman and his patient Dr. Spencer Fifield, a thirty-eight-year-old bachelor internist whose program for his life is a purely intellectual construction. As a satire of people who cannot see others as they are, or establish connections with them, *Vertical and Horizontal* might have fit into Merchant Ivory's ironic world; but after Ross prepared a screenplay for Paramount, the studio never proceeded with the film.

What did come to term for Merchant Ivory was their film *The Guru*. Ivory had been considering the idea for a picture about a celebrated Indian musician and a Western disciple who crystallized as an English rock star shortly after George Harrison of the Beatles went to India in 1966 to study the sitar with Ravi Shankar. When Ivory presented his proposal to 20th Century Fox, studio heads found the conception timely and commissioned a screenplay. Jhabvala provided one quickly, Fox read and liked it and within forty-eight hours authorized Ivory to begin the film. Fox's $860,000 investment in the picture, drawn from rupees earned by Fox in India that could not be taken out of the country, was the largest budget Merchant Ivory had known. Yet everything seemed to go wrong in the making of the movie. On the first day of shooting, Utpal Dutt, who was the Maharaja in *Shakespeare Wallah* and who plays here the key role of the Indian musician-guru, was jailed for having produced Maoist plays in West Bengal, and it seemed virtually impossible to free him. Using every contact he possessed, however, Merchant produced a kind of miracle and won his release. But the company's problems were far from over. People working on the picture did not get along well together, and Michael York's wife Pat became dangerously ill—all of which created a tense, anxious atmosphere in which to work.

Like *Shakespeare Wallah*, *The Guru* deals with the failure of Westerners to merge with Indian culture; but in a way, *The Guru* is the reverse of the earlier film. In *Shakespeare Wallah*, the Westerners feel, rightly or wrongly, that they have something to give—the heaped up treasures of Western civilization; while in *The Guru* they come to India to see what they can get for themselves by way of the culture and spiritual enrichment of the East. Tom Pickle, a famous English rock singer played by Michael York, comes to India to learn the sitar from one of its Indian masters, but for him learning to play the sitar is a musical discipline without its also being a spiritual one. Another young English character, a kind of groupie (Rita Tushingham), has little musical ability but more spiritual openness, and for a time she is enamored of the Indian sitarist. When she falls sick, however, and a fuller sense of the Indian heritage comes to her in terrible nightmares, she wants to go home, cannot deal with such complexity. At the end she and Tom go back to London to be married, and with a nice irony the groupie is united with a musical idol belonging to the safer, more familiar world she knows.

55

(left) Tom Pickle's appallingly crass manager, played by Barry Foster, with the Ustad's groupie Jenny (Rita Tushingham).

(below) Begum Sahiba, the Ustad's eldest wife (Madhur Jaffrey, plotting again), with Mastani (Zohra Segal), a holy woman with special powers for getting rid of girls like Jenny.

(opposite) The Guru's guru (Nana Palsikar) rebukes the Ustad for his worldliness and lack of true seriousness, as an amused Tom Pickle looks on.

The Guru is an agreeable film that is flawed in certain respects. Michael York as Tom lends star presence to the picture, but he seems unwilling to risk any emotions to the point where his coolness becomes a kind of blankness, a failure to respond. Nor can Rita Tushingham as the impressionable Jenny do much with her part; she is always called upon to be wide-eyed and vulnerable, but her lack of real identity, while part of the point of the film, deprives her of any deeply engaging interest. The strength of *The Guru* comes chiefly from its strong Indian cast. Utpal Dutt is splendid as the guru-master of the sitar, Ustad Zafar Khan, whose relationship to his disciple Tom is always ambivalent. In India, Tom finds a restful haven from the pressures of show business but is far from ready to surrender his sense of personal identity formed by the West. Khan reveals a similar conflict: he finds self-forgetfulness

Pickle lounges in the Ustad's music room with—insult of insults!—his shoes on.

58

Utpal Dutt. His (simulated) mastery of
the sitar was helped, he says, by much
practising in prison. He was the first of
Merchant Ivory's actors to be called
upon to impersonate a gifted musician,
and was by far the most dedicated: the
sitar's steel strings cut his fingers,
unprotected by the hard calluses that
normally form on the hands of India's
virtuoso musicians.

to a large degree in the music he plays with such purity, but he is
never really free of worldly vanity. When Tom's crude show-business
manager arrives to tempt his star back to London and a big concert
tour, Khan is tantalized by the thought of such a tour for himself.
He is angered when Indian youths mob Tom for his autograph, which
places celebrity above the self-abnegation required of the master musician, but at the same time he is deeply envious.

An amusing moment in the film's extremely fine comic portrait of
the guru occurs when he visits his own guru, an elderly, impassive
man who rebukes him like a child, telling him that his playing contains
too much flash, attributable to his hobnobbing with foreigners, or perhaps even to drinking. Khan's vanity is seen, too, in his relationship to
his wives; he could, he points out, have four, but has "only two." The
elder of the two, the spirited Madhur Jaffrey in Bombay, has given him
five daughters but no son, a source of discomfiting domestic strife; and
the young wife, Aparna Sen, tucked away in Benares, may be beautiful
but is unhappy in her sequestration. The warring wives, the fruits of
his vanity, keep Khan busy; and one comes to see that the film, finally,
is more about him than the Western visitors. The portrait of Khan is
completed at the end as, a solitary figure, he walks alone along a beach
while the movie credits are shown. He is now intimately known and
fully revealed.

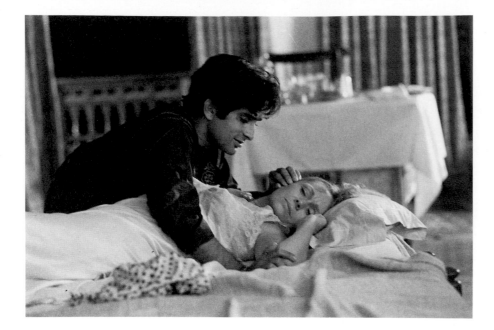

(left) Vikram (Shashi Kapoor) and a depressed Lucia Lane (played by Kapoor's wife, Jennifer Kendal).

(below) Pincho Kapoor as another of the Merchant-Ivory-Jhabvala gurus.

BOMBAY TALKIE
(1970)

MERCHANT ATTRIBUTED *The Guru's* scant success at the box office to Fox's failure to make the additional investment necessary to promote the film. He looked for financing for his next picture, *Bombay Talkie*, not from a major studio but from independent investors. The $200,000 funding for the picture came from a number of individuals, the chief of whom was Joseph Saleh, a Jewish Iraqi businessman and one-time Columbia Pictures executive living in New York who had prospered in real estate and wanted to be in films. He had even, Merchant remarked, "wanted to buy Merchant Ivory Productions, give us a three-year contract and guaranteed income, which was then in some ways quite attractive."

In *The Guru* two musical celebrities belonging to the different cultures of East and West find they cannot come to any accommodation, and their relationship ends in a stalemate. But in *Bombay Talkie* the relationship between the English novelist Lucia Lane (Jennifer Kendal) and the Indian screen star Vikram (Shashi Kapoor) is worse than stalemated, it is decidedly destructive. Humor appears in various parts of the picture—in the opening sequence, an outrageous and entertaining send-up of Indian musical films in which, for instance, performers cavort on the keys of a giant typewriter; in quiet scenes like the one in which an old Indian gentleman with thick, blue-tinted glasses who claims to be a writer appears at Lucia's door to ask her to autograph her novel *Consenting Adults*; and in episodes involving another of Jhabvala's gurus, who plays Ping-Pong gleefully and shows home movies of his celebrity conquest of Los Angeles. But for the most part the film is somber, as it explores the relationship that develops between Lucia and Vikram.

(above left) Lucia Lane, home wrecker, spreads her evil wings.

(above right) Vikram and his barren wife Mala, the actress Aparna Sen.

In certain respects Lucia and Vikram are alike. The novels Lucia writes are daydreams of love and romance for a popular audience in the West, and the films Vikram stars in provide celluloid romance for the Indian masses. Their affair cannot take hold because neither of them has any mooring in reality. In their overdramatized emotions, set against the backdrop of Bombay film sets and kitschy houses that resemble them, their lives belong precisely to a fictional script. In what they do and how they relate to each other, they seem entrapped by the roles they play; they are not free to enter life or to become real—like a situation in Pirandello. Kendal gives a beautifully shaded performance as the picture's lost lady, held under the spell of her own boredom and self-centeredness, and up to a point the movie's conception is interesting. But it has too little substance to sustain it. One does not care much about Vikram, who is too much at the mercy of Kendal's femme fatale, and whose deterioration is too predictable. When ennui threatens, Ivory provides a production number, or bizarre set piece, but these are not enough.

Not all of those nice Merchant Ivory movies conclude cheerfully. *Bombay Talkie* ends with a brutal stabbing. Zia Mohyeddin, who plays Hari, the rival for Lucia's affections, stabbed Kapoor so violently with a collapsible dagger that the "blood" shot up onto the wall over everybody's head.

What makes the film worth watching is a strange kind of intensity that Ivory brings to it. It is felt partly in his fascination with place, with the physical presence of Bombay—from the magnificent, five-storied staircase of the Taj Mahal Hotel to the city's nightscapes in which lonely looking streets are lined with poor people sleeping on the pavements. In a memorable scene Lucia celebrates her birthday by going out late at night in a horse-drawn carriage with Vikram and Hari, Vikram's screenwriter friend and rival for her. The carriage is filled with brightly colored balloons that float free across the dark, deserted streets and are left behind on the paving stones like reminders of the brevity of happiness, while a woodwind instrument sounds a plaintive note. The atmospheric richness of the scene gives an impression of Ivory's reaching out toward a picture of larger and more panoramic scope than he had attempted previously. In this respect, *Bombay Talkie* (which remains one of Ivory's own favorites despite its poor reception) is prophetic, predicting the large evocative canvases that Ivory will later create.

Nirad Chaudhuri and crew at a grand Saville Row–type tailoring establishment in London. This was the first Merchant Ivory film shot by Walter Lassally (*behind camera, far right*).

ADVENTURES OF A BROWN MAN
IN SEARCH OF CIVILIZATION
(1972)

AFTER *BOMBAY TALKIE,* Merchant Ivory turned next to a documentary. BBC television commissioned them to do a film on Nirad Chaudhuri, the celebrated Indian polymath whom Merchant, Ivory, and Jhabvala had all known in India, and who was then in England doing research for a book on the Sanskrit scholar Max Müller. Chaudhuri is clearly an extraordinary man. His interests are not only cross-cultural (he is a brilliant commentator on the comparative cultures of India and the West) but also interdisciplinary— involving history, anthropology, linguistics, political science, sociology, and a half-dozen other fields. He can talk on any subject under the sun. Chaudhuri is also a passionate Anglophile, as he proclaimed in his book *A Passage to England,* one of whose chapter titles provides the title of the documentary.

In the 54-minute film, Ivory observes the diminutive (he is only five feet tall), seventy-six-year-old scholar in the settings of Oxford and London. Ivory places him in a number of situations a dinner party, a don's study, a visit to a graveyard, a fitting at a tailor's, a walk along the town's High Street—and lets him talk. Nimble-witted and voluble, he expounds on everything from the beauties of his beloved Mozart to the misrule, or rather the lack of any rule at all, of India; from his passion for Kipling (the best of all English writers on India, he maintains) to the vacuousness of the yoga cult and the intellectually damaging effects of the Indian diet, deficient in protein. His spryness as a walker of Oxford's streets is matched by his biting and provocative opinions, which he appears to relish. He becomes a self-creating portrait; and Ivory, in fact, regards the film, so concise and yet so full of life, as a "profile."

SAVAGES
(1972)

T HE GENESIS OF the company's next feature film, *Savages*, goes
back to 1970. In an article in the Autumn 1971 issue of the
British film journal *Sight and Sound*, Ivory relates that he came
across a Colonial Revival mansion in Scarborough, forty minutes north
of New York City, that had intrigued him. Called Beechwood, it
belonged to the Vanderlip family, Midwesterners who derived their

(opposite) Beechwood, overlooking the Hudson River.

(right) Paulita Sedgwick and Sam Waterston, the most civilized of the savages.

wealth from railroads and flourished in the earlier part of the century. But by the time Ivory happened onto it, the elder Vanderlip had died, his children had married and moved away, and only a grandson and great grandson still lived, or camped, there. "My accidental discovery of Beechwood," he writes, "led me to the making of *Savages,* though at the time—November 1970—I couldn't have described what sort of film I wanted to shoot in it. There was something a bit unearthly in the ambiance of Beechwood, something poetic, which made it unlike other houses of the kind I'd seen in America, and this strangeness made me think sometimes of a kind of Hudson River *Last Year at Marienbad.*"

At about this time Ivory had been conferring with his friend George Swift Trow, a *New Yorker* staff writer, about a film conception of his that was tentatively called *Stephen's Story.* It had to do with a friend of Ivory's in the late 1950s, Stephen Scher, who after graduating from Yale was studying art history in a graduate program in New York. He lived comfortably on the Upper East Side, and his interest in medieval art was gentlemanly; yet he also worked as an unpaid auxiliary policeman, patrolling Central Park on horseback once a week. As an auxiliary policeman he was able to wear a uniform, ride a horse, carry a nightstick and gun, and, as Ivory says, not without affection, "swagger around in big boots." As Ivory thought about Scher, it seemed to him that there might be an interesting story in his "dual nature," but he could make nothing satisfactory of it. He later showed what he had written to Trow, who produced a scenario that turned the material into a fantasy, but this conception didn't seem right either.

Yet in the course of their conversation one day a new idea came to them influenced by *Exterminating Angel,* Buñuel's film about a group of guests at a dinner party in a wealthy man's mansion who come under a kind of enchantment and revert to a primitive state. Unlike Buñuel's film, however, Ivory and Trow's characters would begin as savages, become civilized briefly, and then become savages again. At this point, Beechwood entered into the conception as the setting of this strangeness. Ivory put the idea to Merchant, who was enthusiastic; and the next day Ivory and Trow, together with Michael O'Donoghue, a young writer brought in by Trow, began work on a screen treatment. It was submitted to Joseph Saleh, principal backer of *Bombay Talkie* who, despite that film's poor showing at the box office, liked the new project and agreed to invest in it.

Eight weeks after Saleh's commitment, the company began shooting at Beechwood, which as their single location helped to keep production costs down. A mostly nonunion crew was used, and actors drawn chiefly from the Broadway and Off-Broadway theater (Sam Waterston, Kathleen Widdoes, Thayer David, and Salome Jens, among others) worked for minimal salaries, through a dispensation that Merchant Ivory received from the Screen Actors Guild because of the production's low budget. Walter Lassally, the renowned British cinematographer whom Merchant Ivory first used on *Adventures of a Brown Man*, also agreed to work for a modest fee and a share of the profits. The most prodigious contributor to the film, however, was Beechwood itself. "It imposed itself on everything," Ivory remarked, "from the actual scene-by-scene construction of the film to the choice of costumes and props." More than all else, Beechwood provided the atmosphere of time standing still. The house had been shuttered shortly before World War II, when the Vanderlip men went into the armed services, and the savages are dressed in the clothes of the 1930s period that stands complete and intact, sealed off from the present.

Savages begins at dawn in black-and-white with a ritual of human sacrifice by a forest tribe of "mud people," who wear loin cloths and large masks. The ritual is suddenly interrupted by the flight of a seemingly charmed sphere, a croquet ball, that lands in their midst. Awed by the unfamiliar object, they search for its source in the woods beyond, discovering the grounds of a great estate lying empty and deserted. As they enter the mansion warily and the film goes into sepia, they stroke its furnishings, lick the surface of an oil portrait, and find clothes in upstairs rooms. By mid-afternoon, and now in color, they have become transformed into wealthy social types of the period between the two world wars. At a formal dinner party in the evening, the guests exchange gossip and speak of business concerns and affairs of state. After midnight, however, their civilized veneer begins to disintegrate and they engage in orgies in the cellar. By dawn of the next day, bringing the twenty-four-hour time scheme full cycle, the guests play croquet on the lawn, go off in pursuit of the balls they have sent flying into the woods and, shedding their clothes as they go, return to their primitive state.

The controlled strangeness of *Savages* is continually beguiling. Typed as savages, the characters remain typed when they become civi-

(opposite above left) The savages discover a top hat and take it for a pretty little drum.

(opposite above right) After-dinner entertainments: Carlotta foretells the future for her guests with the aid of some spoiling peaches.

(opposite below) Screenwriter George Trow *(at the piano)* takes the cast through "Follow the Gleam."

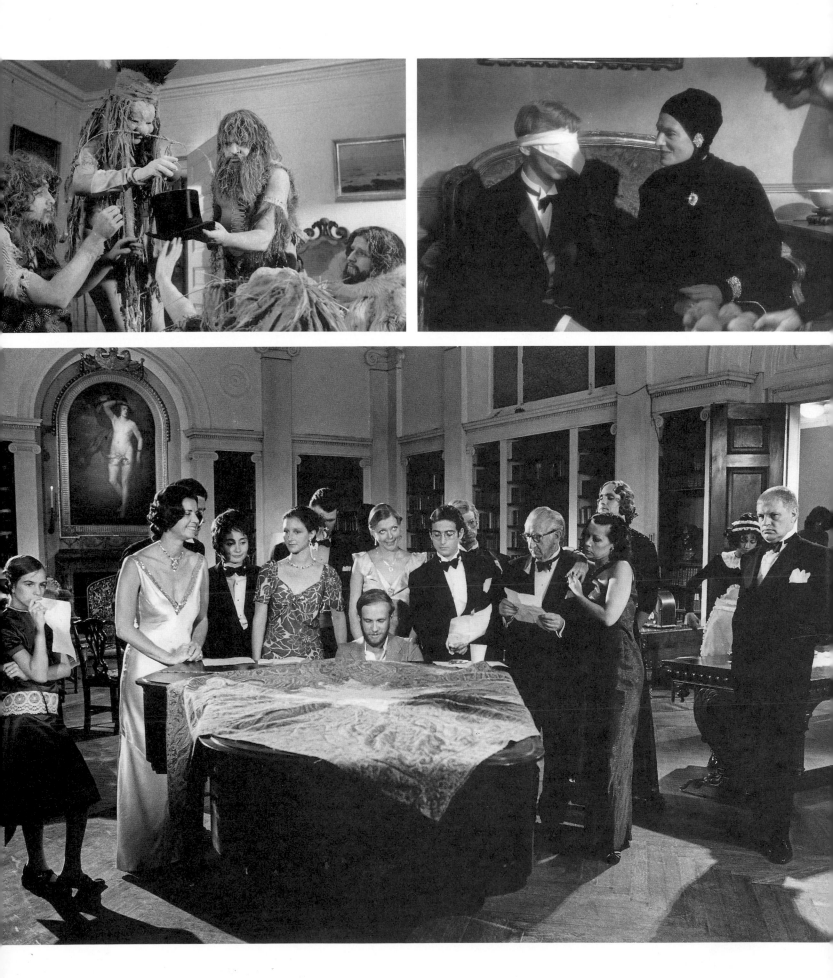

lized. The Limping Man in the forest (a sensitive man who can take no action) becomes the Limping Man in formal attire; the Priestess becomes the Society Matron; the humble Forest Girl is now a Lady's Maid. In the new social roles they play, the characters occasion a good deal of absurdist comedy. At a dinner party, no one seems to notice, or to find it out of place, that a tall, athletic young man wears a dress. The Society Matron asks her guests suddenly and incongruously if they know the meaning and derivation of the word "bric-a-brac"; and Lady Cora and Sir Harry, an elderly couple who have shared a lifetime together, suddenly reveal that they find each other "extraordinarily dull." It is all completely meaningless in a way, yet manages to suggest how fragile and arbitrary the conventions of the "civilized" are, how like they are even to the hierarchical orderings and rituals of mud people. One becomes aware of the civilized characters' vulnerability. At the same time the ambiance of the 1920s and 30s (in the clothing the characters wear, lawn recreations, swimming pool, and gleaming Pierce Arrow automobile standing out on the drive) is effectively evoked. It is re-created alluringly and then, with the savages' departure, vanishes before one's eyes. *Savages* is a witty, richly conjured trompe l'oeil, a trick of time.

The picture has been superbly photographed by Lassally, the cast is consistently good, and the dialogue of Trow and O'Donoghue

(opposite left to right) Susie Blakely, Kathleen Widdoes, Asha Puthli; *(above)* Asha Puthli; *(below)* The Pierce Arrow.

The High Priestess holds aloft the magical croquet ball that is soon to transform her into Carlotta, the society hostess.

is observant and "savagely" funny. Yet the sensibility of Ivory can also be noticed, particularly his concern with the theme of time and transience. His interest in socially delineated figures placed in a context of time and change goes back to his first film, *Venice: Theme and Variations*, and it is brought to near perfection in *Shakespeare Wallah*, in which nostalgia enters in, the poignancy of a lost world. It appears again in *Savages* with an encompassing effect in all the whispered meanings of the vacant Beechwood.

The visual beauty of the sprawling, white frame mansion is almost hypnotic, and Ivory lets the camera take it in at times at a distance, at times close up. It has an idyllic quality, this lost playground of the rich that would have interested F. Scott Fitzgerald. Fantasy is not quite out of place in such a setting. In a fine episode at dusk the guests discover the body of a dead whippet at a far end of the lawn, and gather about it wonderingly, as if with a dawning consciousness of death, as the lights of the house behind them flicker on and off, suggesting some awful power failure. The sense of the impermanence of time is felt again as civilization crumbles and the Song Writer-Poet retires to an upper-story room to play his cello with mournful beauty. *Savages* is a poetic meditation on time, the poignant nostalgia of which has been restrained by a cockeyed kind of drawing-room comedy.

The film, which was financed by Joseph Saleh at a total cost of $350,000, was highly praised when it was shown in England and France, and it was the most talked about film at the 1972 Cannes Film Festival, but its subsequent opening in New York was disappointing. When Merchant and Saleh, who were unable to secure a distributor's advance, opened the film themselves at the Baronet Theater in New York, it received harsh reviews. "It played for five weeks in New York," Ivory comments, "and then vanished." In retrospect, one wonders which was the more remarkable, that it could have been so slighted, or that Merchant Ivory could, in their first American film, have produced a work so original, imaginative, and assured.

CHAPTER IV

The Mid-Seventies
—Time

HELEN, QUEEN OF THE NAUTCH GIRLS
(1973)

*H*ELEN, *QUEEN of the Nautch Girls*, a 30-minute documentary film that looks at an aspect of Indian culture from a rather whimsical angle, has always been a popular Merchant Ivory film. The idea for the documentary came from Anthony Korner, an associate of Merchant Ivory's in this period, and it was directed and narrated by him. But the scenario was devised by Ivory. The subject of the film, which cost a modest $17,000 to make, is the most popular dancer in Bombay musical films—so much so that since 1957 she had appeared in five hundred of them. In part the movie is a montage of scenes from her pictures and of the opening sequence in *Bombay Talkie* in which Helen dances with Shashi Kapoor on the keys of the giant red typewriter. Indian musical films that provided the background of *Bom-*

(opposite) Helen dances over the giant red typewriter in the opening sequence from *Bombay Talkie.*

(below) Helen makes up in her dressing room.

(below right) A still from one of Helen's five hundred films.

bay Talkie now come to life before the bemused viewer. Stepping neatly around the puritanic codes governing Indian films that forbid direct sexual contact (even kissing), the musicals project sexuality fervently through innuendo—in teasing situations and the sensuality of Helen's dancing. Extravagantly romantic fantasies are the stuff of this popular art form, of which Helen is clearly "queen."

Set off against the film clips are scenes in which Helen, in her dressing room and a car traveling across town, talks in the most practical way about her life and future prospects, the likelihood that when she becomes too old for her present roles she will open a boutique with some "nice and groovy" name. Helen the romantic myth confronts Helen the down-to-earth working girl. The dance numbers she performs sometimes involve melodramatic situations that may provoke a smile (in one Helen taunts a black convict locked in a cage who is driven to desperation to get at her); but one's reactions are actually more complicated than this. Helen manages to generate a sense of excitement (at times perhaps even of danger) as the lid of Pandora's box is opened, and the many shapes of forbidden desires and fantasy are released. Reinforced by the surging rhythms of background music, and the camera's powerful concentration on her (and her thrusting pelvis), Helen draws one into a dream world. Korner remembers a private screening of the film in which he turned to see the projectionist blowing kisses at the screen—a tribute to the musicals' naive power. Helen's performances are likely to evoke a mixed reaction: they *do* represent a corruption of traditional Indian art forms, as the narrator claims, yet are undeniably vibrant. Korner and Ivory stand back, drawing the viewer into the spectacle without making any direct comment.

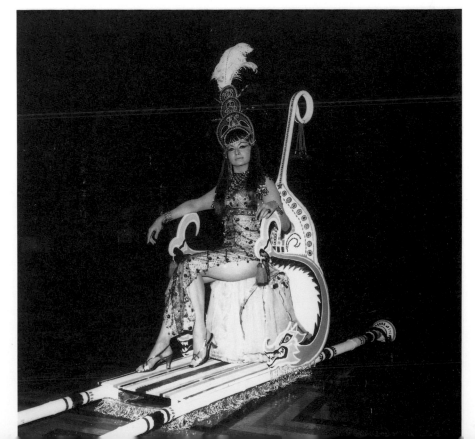

(left) Sajid Khan—the Mad Boy—on Juhu Beach, Bombay.

(opposite) Sajid Khan and friend.

MAHATMA AND THE MAD BOY
(1974)

MERCHANT IVORY'S NEXT FILM, a 27-minute short, was not only produced but for the first time also directed by Merchant. *Mahatma and the Mad Boy,* the idea for which was suggested by Sajid Khan, a child star of Indian films who plays the vagrant boy on a Bombay beach, was filmed in 1973 and received highly favorable reviews when it was shown in London the following year. It cost $25,000 to make and was shot in just five days on Bom-

I had known Sajid Khan from his earlier films in India as a child star, the most famous being *Mother India,* directed by Mehboob Khan, in which he played a five-year-old brat and know-it-all, if a thoroughly captivating one. Sajid came from a very humble background, and his parents had separated. Mehboob Khan and his wife, Sardar Akhtar, took

74

to Sajid and adopted him, though they had other sons. They gave him the attention and love he had not received from his natural parents, and he easily settled into his new, luxurious surroundings.

Within a year or two, American producers, the King Brothers, came to India on behalf of MGM to make the film *Maya*, and they selected Sajid to play the young Indian elephant boy. The film was successful, and MGM continued it as a television series. Sajid was flown to Los Angeles, where he was more or less adopted by yet another family, this time American, and also well-off. He enrolled in Beverly Hills High, and for a time became a famous teenage heartthrob, with an hour-long musical special on ABC and his picture on the covers of teen fan magazines. When he made a publicity tour of Japan, he was mobbed by Japanese girls. His success, however, didn't last long, and he returned to India in the hopes of resuming his film career there. But by now Mehboob Khan had died and Sajid got little work. People in a position to help him in the Indian film industry resented his American success.

He was introduced by me to Sunita Pitambar, in whose grand house we had given our party for Vivian Leigh. Sunita took a great liking to Sajid and ended up adopting him as well. Sajid's fortune—or was it his fate?—was always to be adopted by the very rich. Now about forty, he has probably packed more into his many lives than anyone else I know. Satayjit Ray felt that Sajid was the best natural child actor he'd ever seen, and he ought to know. IM

Moving from producer to director on *Mahatma and the Mad Boy* was a very big switch for me. Throughout the entire filming I constantly thought of production problems and whether things would happen on time so that I could direct the actors and line up the shots. It was a short schedule, only about five days, but during the monsoon season. We were constantly struggling with intermittent showers and capricious tides. The day we completed the shooting we went to the recording studio and, without seeing a frame of the film, recorded the background music—Vivaldi's "Winter" section from *The Four Seasons* performed on Indian instruments, the melody providing a basis for improvisation in the manner of an Indian raga. IM

bay's Juhu Beach, whose Westernized Indians were satirized in *The Guru* and in *Bombay Talkie*. In the time frame of a single day (from dawn to dusk), the film records the wanderings of an Indian youth who sleeps on the beach, holds conversations with a statue of Mahatma Gandhi, and scavenges for food with his monkey. By afternoon, a little ceremony is held by well-to-do Gandhi-ites, at which a speaker delivers a sermon on "godly love"; but when the boy comes too close, he is told to move on by a guard, one of a series of exclusions of this onlooker-outcast.

Tanveer Forooqi's screenplay is perhaps too schematic in its pointed contrast between the complacent "haves" and the solitary, disregarded "have not," but it is effective in its delicate portrait of the estranged boy, always framed by sea and sky. The film is photographed by Subrata Mitra with a gentle lyricism that includes small touches of humor, and it is enhanced by its musical score, selected by Merchant, the "Winter" Concerto from Vivaldi's *Four Seasons*. A quiet mood of regret gives unity to the piece and lingers in the viewer's mind after the final, held shot of the Mad Boy walking alone along the beach. In the brief *Creation of Woman*, Merchant had worked with bold strokes to make a strong impression, but in *Mahatma* he has learned new subtlety and refinement that endow the film with real charm.

AUTOBIOGRAPHY OF A PRINCESS
(1975)

IN 1974 MERCHANT IVORY made two new films, *Autobiography of a Princess* and *The Wild Party*. Although released after *The Wild Party*, *Autobiography of a Princess* was the first to be filmed. It has an intriguing history, which Ivory has related in his book *Autobiogra-*

The cenotaphs of the dead queens. Cyril Sahib (James Mason) describes this in the film as being "more lonely than any other place I know on earth . . . nothing there except a few vultures . . . I thought the cenotaphs themselves resembled vultures. Or some extinct species of bird come to roost in the desert . . . "

(opposite) Madhur Jaffrey. A garlanded portrait of "Papa" hangs above the chimneypiece.

phy of a Princess, a miscellany of commentary and photos of Royal India, together with the text of Jhabvala's screenplay of the film. As Ivory explains, Merchant was in India in 1973 putting together material for a possible documentary that would include archival footage as well as interviews with descendants of the Maharajas. When he accepted an invitation from the former Maharaja of Jodhpur, Ivory and Jhabvala went along. While observing the crew shooting scenes in one of the rooms of the palace, Ivory began to reflect on "what Bai-ji, the Jodhpur princess, had told us in her interview about her life here, about going to school in Switzerland and coming back to Jodhpur, and how everybody had tried to force her into purdah. Suddenly I thought of the actress Madhur Jaffrey: what a princess she would make!"

Back in New York, Ivory corresponded with Jhabvala about his conception for the film, which would incorporate some of Merchant's archival footage but deal centrally with the princess, living in a self-imposed exile in London. By then, Ivory writes, "we had also added another character: Cyril Sahib, an aging Englishman retired from India, a friend of the Princess, sharing her memories—but with a different view of them." A work of barely an hour's length, *Autobiography of a Princess* was produced for Channel 13 television in New York for $70,000.

An abandoned royal bus used for pig-sticking excursions into the desert. Behind it is the modern Umaid Bhavan Palace, started in 1929 by Maharaja Umaid Singh as a public works project during a famine. This was the principal set of *Hullabaloo Over Georgie and Bonnie's Pictures*.

(left) The arrival of the Prince of Wales (later King Edward VIII) at the Bikanir station in 1921.

(opposite) The Fort at Jodhpur.

A brooding Cyril Sahib (James Mason) faces the evidence of his misspent youth in the old film footage that is the heart of *Autobiography of a Princess*.

The picture was filmed in London in just five days, to keep within a tight budget, and makes use of only a few actors, principally Madhur Jaffrey as the princess and James Mason as Cyril Sahib. The casting of James Mason makes a piquant footnote to the making of the film. From the beginning Merchant was convinced that Mason was exactly right for the role. Ivory remarks: "Ismail kept saying 'James Mason. James Mason. Oh, he'll be good. You must try James Mason.' Ruth and I kept saying we weren't sure. Finally he sent him the script and cast him anyway. When we heard about it we were alarmed." Ivory's misgiving was that Mason was too glamorous for the part; and after meeting the dapper Mason for dinner at the Dorchester in London, his worst fears were confirmed. "All that night," he says, "I tossed and turned, thinking I just couldn't go through with this." Yet when Mason arrived for rehearsal, he had become a different person: "grey, nondescript, wearing an old man's sweater, creeping up the stairs, easing himself into a chair. Then he opened his mouth: we didn't need to make a single change. Letter perfect with wonderful pauses."

Observing classical unities, the action of *Autobiography*, which has the single setting of the princess's Kensington apartment, takes place within the hour's length of the picture itself. Its occasion is an annual tea honoring the birthday of the princess's late father. To the apartment comes her friend Cyril Sahib, the sharer of her memories. She has rented a projector and screen and shows film clips of the Maharaja and his circle in the time of the Raj, as the two drink their tea and reveal their souls. Among the first noticed of Jhabvala's multilayered ironies is that while the film clips evoke an expansive, hedonistic past in India, the London apartment gives a sense of constriction and confinement. Dominated by a large portrait of the Maharaja, it seems cluttered and claustrophobic.

Madhur Jaffrey is the perfect princess, a woman of flashing temperament and a dogged obsession with her father, whom she regards almost as a lover. She had been the spoiled darling of his court, and even her out-of-date expressions ("topping," "ripping") suggest that she has never completely outgrown that experience. What gradually emerges, however, is that the Maharaja was a manipulator of those around him, a charming yet cruel man who indulged his whims at the expense of others, and whose later years were soiled by a tawdry London sex scandal that made newspaper headlines. "Papa loved parties and fun," the princess exclaims ecstatically, remembering the past only selectively, forgetting that he had also been responsible for her disastrous arranged marriage. The Maharaja's creature, his legacy to her is placelessness, an inability to come to terms with the past in her life in London where she seems curiously alone.

By the end, however, the film's chief character is Cyril, who, if his fate is also written in the past, understands it better than the princess. His experience is like hers in some ways, since as the Maharaja's one-time tutor he had been a coddled favorite, a kind of ersatz lover (his homosexuality is hinted at) who now lives in a lonely seclusion in Turton-on-Sea. The conscious character of the two, he recognizes that the Maharaja's sybaritic court life had sapped him of his will, left him without direction or purpose. The Maharaja's legacy to him is the loss of a sense of reality. The films that are shown, a montage of brief and confusingly connected moments, become incoherent—just as Cyril's life in India, the longer he stayed, had become. His writing a book on an Englishman in India, Denis Lever, who had dedicated himself to constructive work, seems a form of self-reproach, an attempt to recover some remaining fragments of dignity in old age. Cyril is one of Mason's finest performances, full of weariness and painful memories communicated in a pensive, inwardly searching hesitancy.

Autobiography, which was warmly received when it was shown in England, belongs in large part to Jhabvala. It has the qualities of her tight, ironic fiction in which an unsparing scrutiny of her characters also allows for compassion. It is remarkable both in its economy and its density; and it takes up a theme that occupies Jhabvala in her fiction and Ivory in his films throughout this seventies period, the definition of characters through their relationship to time.

THE WILD PARTY
(1974)

TIME ALSO HAS A framing role in *The Wild Party*, shot soon after *Autobiography*. It has a curious history, having been inspired by a blank-verse narrative poem of 1926 by Joseph Moncure March about a disastrous Greenwich Village party given by a vaudeville comic in his walk-up apartment. The lyricist Walter Marks saw in it the idea for a musical film, with the setting changed to Hollywood at the end of the silent-movie era. Shortly after the project was brought before Edgar Lansbury and Joseph Beruh, producers of *Godspell* and other Broadway musicals, Walter Marks's brother Peter discussed it with Ivory and mentioned that a director was needed. It was in this way that Ivory, as director, and Merchant, as coproducer with Lansbury and Beruh, were brought in. An important change was made in the script on which Ivory and Marks collaborated: the musical became a drama with music.

The Wild Party was shot on location during May and June 1974, at the Mission Inn, at Riverside, in southern California. The Mission Inn, a hotel built in 1895, is a strange assemblage of architectural styles (mostly Spanish Moorish) with cloisters, chapels, galleries, bell towers, flying butresses, and a magnificent spiral staircase. Evocative of Hollywood in the 1920s, it became the mansion of the silent-film comic Jolly Grimm (James Coco) and his mistress Queenie (Raquel Welch). The casting of Raquel Welch happened practically by chance, since Ivory had not necessarily been looking for a big star. "I saw the 'Today Show,'" Ivory recalls, "and Raquel was on. She seemed intelligent and

(opposite) Queenie (Raquel Welch) during a song-and-dance routine, "Singapore Sal."

(right) Queenie with Dale Sword (Perry King) in another dance number, "The Herbert Hoover Drag." The film was referred to by a critic as being the first dark musical, as in *noir*.

(below) Jimmy Coco.

interesting, and she said she'd like to do comedy and wanted to play different roles than she'd been playing, so we sent her the script."

Working with her, however, proved difficult. She came with her own entourage, including her drama coach, and expected special courtesy. When Ivory would compliment her on a scene she would walk away without answering, as if she did not believe him. Then came the day when he wanted another take of a scene that he found "just a little bit boring," and Welch walked off the set, demanding an apology before the assembled cast and crew as the price of her returning. Ivory was to stand up before everyone and more or less say: "Raquel, I'm so sorry that I offended you tonight." Merchant was appalled, but Ivory coolly agreed to do it. The cast and crew gathered in a semicircle, camera lights were turned on, Raquel Welch appeared in a black satin robe and said: "Well, Mr. Ivory, I think you have something to say to me." Ivory gave his apology. Shooting resumed.

More serious problems plagued Merchant Ivory after the film was completed. American International Pictures, which had financed the $750,000 production and was its distributor, did not like Ivory's cut and recut the film to give it, they hoped, more box-office appeal. The AIP version shown in America in 1974 pleased neither audiences nor critics; and when it was set for release in England, Ivory sent a letter to British reviewers protesting that the "wreck that is about to be released in London as my work . . . is the distributor's cheap attempt to exploit everything exploitable." Discarded sex scenes, he pointed out, were put back in; weak episodes that had been eliminated were used; flashbacks and flashforwards were introduced that disrupted the flow of the film; and Jolly Grimm, instead of being a complicated character (bitter, frightened, and violent in his frequent drunks), is made to seem through cutting to be a merely lovable one. Some years later Merchant

Ivory bought back the British rights to the movie, which has been shown in its original version since 1981.

The Wild Party almost inevitably brings to mind the Fatty Arbuckle scandal of 1921, in which the silent-film comic gave a party at his San Francisco hotel suite that ended with the death of a young actress and his sensational trials for murder. But Ivory's film does not resemble the Arbuckle case in any significant way. A fading silent-film comic, Carlo Grimmaldi, using the oxymoronic stage name of Jolly Grimm, plans a comeback with a film he has produced, directed, starred in, and financed himself. Setting the stage for the picture's hoped-for release, he gives a large party at his mansion for Hollywood people at which the film is screened. Everything goes wrong (it is evident that the picture is a failure), and when Jolly's mistress, whom he has mistreated publicly and privately, goes off to a bedroom with Dale Sword, a handsome, rising young star in talkies, his mounting desperation culminates with his shooting both the young man and Queenie herself.

Richly photographed, again by Walter Lassally, *The Wild Party* is set in 1929, as one era ends and another begins that shatters illusions of the past. One of Ivory's strategies is to have envisioned Jolly's experience as a reflection of his own films: the movie comic becomes a real-life player, like Vikram in *Bombay Talkie,* in a tragic melodrama. One comes to see that he had succeeded in his silent films because he really believed in their sentimental innocence. His sentimental susceptibility is brought out in the beguiling little lame girl in his picture whom Jolly, playing an early-day friar, miraculously cures, and in Nadine, the little "Gish girl" who does a dance at the party that fills Jolly's eyes with tears. The musical numbers underscore his idealization of another girl, Queenie, the mainstay of his emotional life. But his relationship to Queenie is at best fragile. Contrasting with Jolly's desperate idealizations is a Hollywood of transitory stardom where sex is anything but innocent, as can be seen in the guests at Jolly's party—the decadent young people and the lecherous producer Kreutzer, whose tiny eyes seem always to be squinting behind Coke-bottle-thick glasses.

When it comes to Jolly that not only his film career but also his relationship to Queenie is coming apart, he goes to pieces. In an early musical number Queenie had stroked her legs and breasts enticingly with a large powder puff, and late in the movie with a kind of recall of that number, Jolly goes into Queenie's bedroom where, at her dressing table with its large powder box, he dabs powder on his face—but too heavily, so that it leaves a stark impression on his cheeks and nose that makes him look like a clown. At this moment, reminiscent of the grotesque ending of *The Blue Angel,* Jolly becomes a tragic clown. In a sense he is the fool of time, which takes from him his very identity.

The film, however, contains a troubling problem for the viewer, because Ivory's detachment and irony permit no sense of identification with Jolly; and, without an identification with at least someone, the film has no emotional center. The viewer remains outside the film, uncertain of what he should be feeling. *The Wild Party* incorporates

Queenie, in her chorus girl days.

Jolly improvises a new action sequence
for his Brother Jasper picture, in the
hope of attracting potential backers.

a theme, the nostalgic loss of an ideal, that had appeared in Ivory's
work as early as *Shakespeare Wallah*, but unlike the Buckinghams,
actors whose time has passed, one can only wonder at Jolly's emotions
without being able to enter into them. The film, though, has redeeming
features, not least of which are James Coco as an ideally cast Jolly
Grimm and Raquel Welch in her best modulated role in films; and
a solid supporting cast that includes Royal Dano as a one-time silent-
film actor and now Jolly's loyal friend and chauffeur, Regis J. Cordic
and Dena Dietrich as the producer and his wife whom Jolly attempts
desperately to interest in his film, and Perry King as the handsome,
synthetic new star Dale Sword (a name that Ivory says came to him in
a dream). There are many very sensitive scenes, the musical production
numbers are polished until they shine, and Ivory's period reconstruction of Hollywood at the end of the twenties is an intriguing backdrop
for Jolly's dispossession.

Mannes College instructor Jean Whitlock with three of her aspiring musicians.

SWEET SOUNDS
(1976)

IN 1976 JHABVALA made the important decision to leave India to live in New York for most of the year, a result of which was a new documentary, *Sweet Sounds*, conceived and directed by Richard Robbins, and sponsored by Merchant Ivory Productions. Jhabvala entered her youngest daughter Firoza, an aspiring pianist, in the Mannes College of Music, then on Manhattan's Upper East Side, and there met Robbins, Firoza's piano teacher and the acting director of the college's preparatory school. Before long Jhabvala introduced him to Merchant and Ivory, a meeting that proved fateful, since, beginning with *The Europeans* in 1978, Robbins has provided the musical scores for nearly all of Merchant Ivory's films. Robbins had an idea for a short film showing some of the small children at the school being initiated into the practice of music, a conception that Merchant and Ivory found engaging. In July 1976, at a cost of $25,000, the 29-minute film was shot at the school; and in the autumn it was shown at the New York and London film festivals, as well as on PBS television.

The documentary begins in a pleasant classroom where two teachers begin instruction of their five-year-old charges into the rudiments of music, and moves by the end to a performance stage. In between, the scene frequently shifts as the children are an audience to the playing of others, then are performers themselves. Part of the charm of the film is the greatness of the undertaking for the children; one sees a vast world open before them, and often their faces are a study, at times impassive, at others revealing, of their uncertainties or aroused interest. The focus of the film shifts from the two teachers who have an infectious enthusiasm for music to the youngsters themselves, who dominate the work. A Chinese girl plays the piano while the small children listen, the camera stealing over their expressive faces; a small boy, John, bows a cello with earnest musicianship. At the end a musical program is presented by five adolescents, while in the audience a little girl is caught by the camera squirming restlessly in her chair, and a boy named Andrew puffs out his cheeks like a bellows and switches his eyes from side to side. In *Sweet Sounds*, in which no direct comment is ever made by Robbins, the youngsters are as fresh and natural as Truffaut's kids.

The Roseland Ballroom. (1977)

ROSELAND
(1977)

MERCHANT IVORY'S NEXT feature film, *Roseland*, also came about by happenstance. Ivory became interested in filming Jhabvala's recently published short story "How I Became a Holy Mother," about an Indian guru who has ironic and satirical affinities with show business. He conducts a tour abroad, and an Indian youth and unlikely English girl from his ashram are exhibited as his spiritual stars. Jhabvala prepared a script (in which the girl becomes an American and the action is set in Oregon), while Merchant sought the financial backing of two brothers, Denis and Michael Murphy, businessmen in Portland, Oregon whose family had prospered in lumber, and who wanted to invest in movies. The Murphys, however, were not enthusiastic about the script and the project fell through. Yet a brief scene planned for the movie, at New York's famous dance palace Roseland, led to the idea for another film that the Murphys agreed to back. Don De Natale, who played the Apache Dancer in *The Wild Party*

(left) The quartet from the "Hustle" segment of the film: (left to right) Geraldine Chaplin, Joan Copeland, Christopher Walken, Helen Gallagher.

(below) Don De Natale, the Roseland MC and something of a kindly Angel of Death, who whirls his fallen dancers into Paradise.

and was also Roseland's part-time MC, prodded Merchant into spending time at the dance pavilion. In turn, Merchant brought along Ivory and Jhabvala, and the conception of a film set there gradually evolved. Jhabvala spent weeks at Roseland, absorbing its atmosphere and talking to people who frequented it, before preparing her script, a bitter-sweet trilogy of people who find in Roseland a private dream world.

Except for a few moments outside the building—mostly scenes of cold, wintry streets—the film takes place wholly at the dance hall. Using Roseland, however, involved a number of problems. Some scenes occurring off the dance floor could be shot during the day when Roseland was closed to the public, but the dance floor scenes had to be filmed at night when the floor was crowded with couples. Because Roseland gave permission to shoot these scenes only on Wednesday night (second-biggest night after Saturday), Ivory had to crowd a tremendous number of the dance floor scenes into a short space of time.

His biggest problem, however, involved unions. The scenic artists' local demanded that he hire a scenic artist and an art director, but because Roseland had forbidden them to make any changes in the dance hall (not so much as to move a curtain, paint a wall, or even change the pink-tinted light bulbs thought flattering to the elderly clientele), there was no need for them. When the scenic artists' union threw up a picket line around Roseland that was joined by members of the Teamsters' Union, however, Merchant Ivory had to compromise by hiring a scenic artist and art director who performed no function and, as Merchant remarks, "sat twiddling their thumbs." Other problems developed over their use of extras. The Screen Actors Guild (SAG) felt that they were using too many Roseland regulars in too prominent a way and required them to sign a contract stipulating that they would never show a non-SAG extra in a close-up or medium shot with a SAG actor—a

Lou Jacobi and Teresa Wright, as Stan and May in the "Waltz" segment of *Roseland*.

condition that Ivory found "ludicrous." Including settlements with unions, the film's production cost came finally to $375,000.

Roseland is made up of three vignettes, rather like short stories, about characters who come to Roseland to find a romance otherwise missing in their lives or to sustain the memory of one from the past. The first, featuring Teresa Wright as a widow bound by memories of her late husband, and Lou Jacobi, a somewhat crude but vital man who offers her a chance for happiness in the present, is essentially a curtain raiser. The final piece, about an aging Viennese woman set on winning the Peabody dance competition, despite warnings that the dance had proven fatal to others of her age, makes a stronger impression, largely because of the splendid performances of Lilia Skala and David Thomas. Stout, tireless, and dominating, Skala makes an amusing contrast to her thin, elderly beau who is unable to keep up with her, is quickly winded on the dance floor and has to sit down to catch his breath. The two old-timers who go onto the dance floor in the shadow of death are sketched with humor and compassion.

The middle and best segment, appropriately called "The Hustle," deals with an ingratiating but slippery gigolo (Christopher Walken) who is admired by a dance instructor (Helen Gallagher), kept by a rich older woman (Joan Copeland), and desired by another woman (Geraldine Chaplin) who must decide between a life of loneliness or one of doubtful solace with the Walken character. Written with understated insight into the characters and directed with deft attention to nuance, *Roseland* is a meditation on the perils and ironies of romance. *Roseland*, which premiered at the 1977 New York Film Festival, where it received a long ovation, is an unusual film for Jhabvala, having more sentiment in it than is customary for her. It is a rather gentle film, but Lilia Skala, David Thomas, Christopher Walken, Helen Gallagher, and Geraldine Chaplin make it memorable.

89

HULLABALOO OVER GEORGIE AND BONNIE'S PICTURES
(1978)

Shri Narain (Saeed Jaffrey) tries to interest two hard-to-please Western collectors, *(above left)* Clark Haven (Larry Pine) and *(above right)* Lady Gee (Peggy Ashcroft).

AFTER INTERVIEWING JHABVALA on BBC television, the producer Melvyn Bragg approached Merchant Ivory with a proposal that they make a film for his new London Weekend Television arts program "The South Bank Show." The subject was open, so long as it had an arts connection. Ivory was receptive, and the subject of collecting Indian miniature paintings, an interest of his since *The Sword and the Flute*, was eventually decided on. The film that resulted, *Hullabaloo Over Georgie and Bonnie's Pictures,* cost £250,000 to make, with finance coming chiefly from London Weekend Television. The script, written by Jhabvala, working closely with Ivory, proved intractable at many points, and Jhabvala would have withdrawn but for Merchant's insistence that they see it through. Difficulties were increased by the fact that the screenplay was still being written when shooting began in India. "We just kept shooting from these random bits of paper," Ivory explains, "and hoped for the best. We were still trying to figure out the denouement on location at the Unmaid Bhawan Palace in Jodhpur." Its improvisatory nature, however, does not show whatever in the finished work, which appeared first on British television and then as a feature film in London that received enthusiastic reviews.

To a young Maharaja's palace come two rival Western art collectors—Clark Haven (Larry Pine), an American private collector and heir to a peach-canning fortune, and Lady Gwyneth McLaren Pugh

Bonnie (Aparna Sen), as one of her royal ancestors kept in purdah.

(Peggy Ashcroft), known as Lady Gee, the buyer for a London museum. They suspect that the Maharaja has a collection of priceless Indian miniature paintings and want to acquire it by whatever means. The Maharaja (Victor Banerjee) believes that the art treasures, even though exposed to rot and decay in a storage room, should remain in the palace where they belong; while his sister (Aparna Sen) can see the advantages of selling the collection. Lady Gee sets her attractive young traveling companion Lynn (Jane Booker) on the Maharaja in an attempt to win him over, while Haven curries favor with the Maharaja's sister. In the background stands the curator of the collection (Saeed Jaffrey), who is also dealing in pictures on the side and gives the impression that he may have some tricks up his sleeve.

As Haven and Lady Gee spar and manipulate, the Maharaja weaves

91

Georgie (Victor Banerjee) distributes Christmas treats while keeping an eye on his plotting houseguests.

stratagems of his own. The collection is seemingly destroyed in a fire, but its destruction later turns out to be a ruse of the Maharaja's; and by the end the characters are back where they were at the beginning, except that the attitudes of Haven and Lady Gee have changed. Having suffered the loss, or apparent loss, of the paintings, they have been brought closer together in a common perception that art has its own inviolability, that the paintings should, after all, remain where they are. Despite its well-defined social comedy, *Hullabaloo* has the quality of a fairy tale that ends with a sense of blessing and reconciliation. Lady Gee remembers a young English girl (the "ghost" of the house) who, as a guest at the palace in the 1920s, had disappeared after a splendid dance and was found dead in a palace car the next morning. She says that she likes to think the girl died from "an excess of happiness," a reflection of her own cherished memory of the palace in former days. The past—felt partly in the paintings themselves, twice

The girl who, Lady Gee tells us, dies from an "excess of happiness"—too irrational a concept for even the most romantic man to swallow.

(overleaf) View from the ramparts of the Jodhpur Fort over the unpromising landscape the original inhabitants came to call "The Region of Death." (1978)

gorgeously unveiled by Ivory—is able here to lift the characters into a vision of wholeness and harmony.

Hullabaloo contains delightfully wry comic moments (even the names of the Maharaja and his sister, Georgie and Bonnie, conferred on them by their Scottish nanny, suggest the playful spirit of the film) and many fine performances, particularly those of Peggy Ashcroft and Saeed Jaffrey. But what is most remarkable about the picture is that it manages to suggest so much with such economy. The intruders who think of art in terms of possession are reminiscent of Henry James in tales like "The Aspern Papers"; and there is something Jamesian about the film's interest in manners, and in the sense it gives of coming out of culture and of belonging to culture. Its weight is light, but it has much grace and perception that, like Merchant Ivory's best films of this period, bring its characters to life and reveal their quandaries in the context of time.

CHAPTER V

The Late Seventies–Early Eighties
—Society

(above) The Wentworth House.

(opposite) Gertrude Wentworth descends from her gazebo.

THE EUROPEANS
(1979)

HULLABALOO OVER GEORGIE and *Bonnie's Pictures*, with its Jamesian commentary on art and acquisitiveness, was followed the next year by *The Europeans*, Merchant Ivory's first adaptation of James. In college, Ivory had read a few of James's works—*The Turn of the Screw, Washington Square*, "The Aspern Papers"—but his real introduction to him came through Jhabvala. "Ruth was astonished to know," he told me, "that I hadn't read any more of his works than I had—but I hadn't. She gave me *The Europeans*. 'Start with this,' she said, 'you can't help but like it,' and then she said, 'In a way he was writing for *you*.' And so I read *The Europeans*, and I really did enjoy it—it was a very good book. That was in 1966, I think. And about '74 we began to develop it as a screenplay. We made it in '78. I was fiddling around with it as a screenplay myself in the beginning, and then Ruth took over."

The Europeans was shot on location in New England, partly in the Salem of Emerson and Hawthorne, in the autumn of 1978. Financing proved a problem. Hoping to present *The Europeans* on Public Television, Merchant Ivory applied for partial funding to the National Endowment for the Humanities, with a supporting endorsement of

Jim used to watch BBC Television productions of Henry James and mutter, "I can do better than that," and "Why should the English be doing this sort of thing, and never the Americans?" The answer became clear after every American financier we approached had turned down *The Europeans*, and it was the English, ironically, who came to our rescue in far-off New Hampshire, sending enough money to make the movie decently. Even though it was a hit on both sides of the Atlantic—a modest hit, but a hit nonetheless—it hasn't been any easier for us to sell Henry James to a major American distributor. But then, James in his lifetime had few passionate admirers in America, and found admiration, then fame, in Europe.

But there was another irony for us when *The Europeans* was picked as the sole British entry in competition at Cannes, and the British film establishment then disowned it. Though principally financed by England's National Film Finance Corporation, it

Jhabvala's script from James's biographer Leon Edel. Yet both Merchant Ivory and Edel were rebuffed by NEH panelists who, incomprehensibly, held that *The Europeans* "was one of James's poorest novels." In fact, no support for the project could be found anywhere in America, despite the most diligent search by Merchant. Support came rather from England's National Film Finance Corporation, which made a substantial commitment. Other investors then lined up behind it, including West Germany's television production company Polytel. At the last moment, however, one of the backers withdrew, and Merchant managed to come up with the shortfall only as the cameras were beginning to roll. The picture, which cost in all about $700,000 to make, was their first to find a significant movie-house audience both in America and abroad.

James's subtle and superbly witty *Europeans* is a comedy of transatlantic manners occasioned by the arrival of a brother and sister, reared abroad, in the rural precincts of Boston in the mid-1840s, where they are taken in by their cousins, the Wentworths, who have been raised to a standard of simple probity and distrust of worldly life. "Wicked," pleasure-loving Europe arrives, with comic effect, on the New Englanders' doorstep. The brother and sister, Felix Young and Eugenia, the Baroness Münster, are each drawn romantically to a member of the Wentworths' circle. Felix, a fledgling artist, eventually marries Gertrude Wentworth, the rebellious daughter; but Eugenia is

had, after all, been made in New England from a book by an American author, directed by an American, produced by an Indian, with a mostly American cast and many American crew members. It was not British enough. But the French selection committee insisted on British nationality; it was a minor skirmish in the long history of battles great and small between France and England. This battle was finally won by the French: they *needed* an English film, and they had plenty of American ones already. Our poster of Lee Remick in a billowy white dress kept being mysteriously pulled down every night from the official British booth on the Croisette, and we would have to put it back up again in the morning. This kind of skulduggery—if such it was—always goes on at film festivals. IM

Gertrude (Lisa Eichhorn) disappoints her tiresome suitor, the clergyman Mr. Brand (Norman Snow).

Mr. Brand again, now united with Charlotte Wentworth (Nancy New)

stymied in her would-be romance with Robert Acton, the most eligible bachelor of the area, who concludes that, with her artful manners, she cannot be trusted. Two weddings are celebrated at the end of the novel—Gertrude's to Felix, and her sister Charlotte's to the Unitarian minister Mr. Brand; but the complicated Eugenia cannot fit into New England's cramped frame; she packs her bags and leaves for Europe.

Jhabvala's screenplay of *The Europeans*, which is one of her finest, is faithful to the novel while making certain skillful changes that accommodate it to the medium of film. She creates a scene, for example, of a ball at the Acton house at which Eugenia begins to recognize that she has no place there, neither with the demure old women (almost crones) who sit in a room off to the side, nor on the dance floor where young couples whirl to a rowdy polka. Jhabvala also provides a new ending in which, as Eugenia prepares to leave in a carriage that Acton puts at her disposal (ironically, what he offers her is a passage out), Mr. Brand and Charlotte joyously speak lines from a book of sermons. The closing image of Mr. Brand and Charlotte captures touchingly the innocent tone of early New England, yet also suggests a narrowness in New England's exclusions.

The movie's cast includes Lee Remick as Eugenia (not as "foreign" or ambiguous as in James but attractive and sympathetic); Tim Woodward as the gentlemanly bohemian Felix; Lisa Eichhorn (much praised by reviewers) as Gertrude; Nancy New as Charlotte; Robin Ellis as Robert Acton, the mercantile New Englander with a troubled conscience; Norman Snow as the Reverend Brand, always garbed in Puritan black; Tim Choate as the attractive, very mildly wayward son Clifford; and Wesley Addy as Mr. Wentworth, who ponders his "moral grounds" with dry humorlessness and is one of the film's chief delights. They give nicely nuanced performances in key with Jhabvala's quiet realism and humor.

The most nuanced performance, however, is that of Ivory. *The Europeans* is not a lyrical novel, but Ivory has exercised his director's prerogative of envisioning the work in his own terms, partly through the scenic arts and with a persistent strain of lyricism in the film's imagery. Continually fascinated by houses, Ivory has found a remarkable one in the Wentworths' large white frame home that is both imposing and simple, and whose spacious grounds make it seem isolated from the world. The Wentworth house becomes the frame for the film, together with another structure, a gazebo in the woods nearby. Approached by an extremely steep flight of steps strewn with autumn leaves, the gazebo suggests the idea of a kind of skeletal Gothic church. It is where Gertrude goes to commune with nature and indulge her imaginative life, and where the artist Felix first appears before her. The New England countryside in autumn is stunning in its beauty but is not included for its own sake. In its sensuous appeal to the pleasure in life, it is the countertheme to the New Englanders' world that, however admirable, is lived essentially indoors, under lock and key (the close-up of the large brass lock and key of the Actons' front door is revealing).

Gertrude is introduced into the giddy and hedonistic world of her cousin, Felix.

The visually lyric qualities of the film are reinforced evocatively by the musical score of Richard Robbins in his first feature film collaboration with Merchant Ivory. Beginning with his documentary *Sweet Sounds* in 1976, Robbins had come to know Merchant, Ivory, and Jhabvala quite well, and he was particularly close to Merchant, who, of the three partners, was the most deeply interested in music. When *The Europeans* was being developed, Merchant suggested that they have Robbins provide its musical score—in this case selecting the music to be used. At his house in upstate New York, I asked Robbins in detail about his long-term collaboration with Merchant Ivory, and about his contribution to *The Europeans*.

Even before the film was shot, he told me, he had thought about the music he would select for it. "I had heard Clara Schumann's Trio, Opus 17 years and years before that project," he remarked, "and its slow movement always seemed to me strikingly beautiful in a special way. When the project came along, it struck me as the right period of time and the right place for it." Eugenia plays the slow movement on the piano when she is at home, expecting Robert Acton to call on her,

Dangerous influences: Felix Young (Tim Woodward) *(above left)* and his sister, the Baroness Münster (Lee Remick) *(above right).*

(right) The Wentworth and Acton families return from church to find a suspicious—or is it intriguing?—interloper in their parlor; *(left to right)* Tim Choate, Nancy New, Norman Snow, Wesley Addy, Robin Ellis, Kristan Griffith.

and it seemed to Robbins fitting for her in many ways. It belonged to European culture and was also composed by a woman whose music was then being heard; it suited Eugenia's background and feelings, as an assertive but sensitive character. The Schumann piece suggested, too, Robbins felt, "the special, almost fairy-tale quality of *The Europeans* that puts you back into a beautiful, distant, idealized past."

In the larger scheme, Robbins believed that the story's contrast between European and American cultures ought to be reflected in a European kind of music and an American kind of music—with, as he remarked, "romantic European feeling on one side, the *high* romantic world that Eugenia has left, and the American world to which she comes that is, I think, much more naive, much less direct about romantic feeling, much more controlled. 'Shall We Gather by the River' is the one exception to that, principally because of its soaring melodic line. Still, there is a kind of naive quality to that, too. All of the Stephen Foster is very simple in its directness: his arrangements were enormously popular in America in the 1840s and 50s. We took the orchestrations directly from the Smithsonian and re-created them—the same instrumentation, the same number of instruments. We tried to be as accurate as we could." *The Europeans* proved to be a particularly happy experience for Robbins. "It was a great beginning for me," he said, "because it gave me a chance to learn about writing for strictly visual elements that support musical ideas rather than trying to deal with large amounts of dialogue."

One of the fascinating features of *The Europeans* is its seemingly effortless blending of visual images of great purity with Robbins's fresh and original yet wonderfully apt choices of music to go with them. *The Europeans* is filled with memorable and beautifully framed scenes of many kinds. One thinks, for example, of when, to the music of a period music box (actually discovered in the house supposed to be Eugenia's), Felix and Gertrude dance together in Felix's studio, whose windows let in a flood of sunlight; and of another scene in which, rather than attending church on a Sunday morning, they steal off into the woods while the refrain of "Shall We Gather by the River" is heard in the background. An especially fine central scene occurs when Eugenia calls on old Mrs. Acton (Helen Stenborg) in her upstairs bedroom. Mrs. Acton has a great face, plain but with a certain beauty in its humanity, and is treated with a measured tenderness. She recommends Emerson's essays to Eugenia haltingly as "improving," a token of her simple faith in high ideals and plain living that is becoming slightly out-of-date as New England begins to enter a more commercial age.

One of the motifs of James's novel and Ivory's film is that the New England scene is not static, as it might seem, but already beginning to move into the future. Lizzie Acton (Kristan Griffith) may have a remarkable resemblance to her mother facially but has a sureness about her that the elder woman lacks; she is a girl in full possession of her territory, outflanking Eugenia in her attempt to win her brother

The Wentworths search their hearts and ponder new developments during evening prayers, while the over-excited Gertrude (*far right*) scribbles a poem.

(overleaf) Eugenia (Lee Remick) rides out into an American landscape few Europeans then—as now—could imagine.

(whom she wants to keep for herself). The new American girl out-maneuvers the European lady. The irony in this is that Eugenia is rejected by Acton for being artful and designing, as if his sister were not. Another irony is that Acton should put such stress on honesty while he does not practice it. He finds Eugenia out in a romantic lie, but does so through a lie of his own as he plies Clifford for incriminating information about her. And is it really Eugenia's lie that decides Acton to reject her or his own inability to act in a sexual and romantic situation? What Acton reveals most is the self-deception of self-conscious virtue. That Eugenia is in the end barred from the Acton house, that Acton cannot act on his natural feelings and impulses, make the New England scene a flawed idyll. Disillusioned by her experience of Europe, Eugenia at first believes that she can come home to a world of perfect innocence, only to learn that there is no place for her. Her fate is to be suspended between the limitations of Europe and of the New World, the nostalgic innocence of which she may long for but not possess. In *The Europeans,* which everywhere has distinction, she is another of Merchant Ivory's displaced characters, baffled in their attempt to claim an elusive ideal.

THE FIVE FORTY-EIGHT
(1979)

IN 1979, SHORTLY AFTER *The Europeans* was completed, Ivory took on an assignment outside Merchant Ivory Productions. One day at lunch he heard that Channel 13 television in New York was doing three adaptations of John Cheever stories for the "Great Performances" series, and that one of them, "The Five Forty Eight," adapted by Terrence McNally, had no director. Ivory then approached them and persuaded them to have him direct it. *The Five Forty Eight*, drawn from a Cheever story about the fictional New York suburb of Shady Hill, concerns an advertising man, John Blake (Laurence Luckinbill), who is emotionally estranged from his wife and those around him. His disturbed secretary, Miss Dent (Mary Beth Hurt), whom he has seduced and then fired and discarded, pursues him harrowingly, and in a final scene in which she holds him at gunpoint in a field beyond the Shady Hill railroad station, she forces him to confront the squalor of his life.

If Wentworth in *The Europeans* was anxious to establish his "moral grounds," Blake has lost all sense of them. His twentieth-century urban and suburban environment seems anomic. At the opening the Blake house is shown; it is a substantial upper-middle-class brick house with white window shutters and a swimming pool, but spiritually it is vacant. A commuter train links Blake with New York City, where he works in a synthetic, claustrophobic office, and is elsewhere seen in the streets near Grand Central Station that give a sense of anonymity. Ivory directs the film, which he calls a "mystery," with a close, steady observation of the characters, paying particular attention

It was necessary to convince the producers that I could direct a thriller. Up to then I'd only made films about India, always described (and I think rightly) by *The New York Times* as comedies, or else very oddball movies about the United States, like *Savages, The Wild Party,* and *Roseland.* I had no real credentials and no better argument than that it would be "fun" (for me). But then, Channel 13 must not have had any real reason *not* to give me the job; so, in the end, they did. JI

to faces—Blake's, which is haggard, and Miss Dent's, which is at moments beautiful, then distorted into a clenched grimness. The style of *The Five Forty Eight* is naturalistic yet has a strong dreamlike quality.

I asked Ivory what had concerned him more in the film, its social background or mystery. "The upper-middle-class lifestyle of the suburbs," he said, "may be interesting to John Updike, who is a master at showing it, and Cheever, who was a master at showing it. But it isn't really interesting, I think." What concerned him more was "the demented woman and her thought processes and what she did." *The Five Forty Eight*, which could hardly be more different from *The Europeans*, is very modern in its urban realism and mood of obsession, something surprising from a director we thought we knew.

(opposite and below) Miss Dent (Mary Beth Hurt) lays siege to her former employer, John Blake (Laurence Luckinbill).

JANE AUSTEN IN MANHATTAN
(1980)

THE ORIGINS OF *Jane Austen in Manhattan*, also set in New York, go back to the sale of the manuscript of Jane Austen's childhood play, based on Samuel Richardson's novel *Sir Charles Grandison*, at a Sotheby's auction in London. The manuscript was acquired by David Astor, owner of the *Observer* newspaper, who was quickly approached by the London Weekend Television arts program "The South Bank Show," apparently without actually seeing it, for production rights. Melvyn Bragg, who had coproduced *Hullabaloo* for the program and was at a party for its screening with Merchant and Ivory, mentioned to them that LWT had just acquired an option on the play. Also without having seen the play, they enthusiastically agreed to do the film version. When Ivory received a photocopy of the manuscript, however, he discovered that it "wasn't a complete play, just this childish thing." Yet Jhabvala felt that it could be used as the "seed" for a film in which theatrical groups compete to acquire and produce the Austen play. After *The Europeans* was made, she prepared the screenplay for *Jane Austen in Manhattan*, and in January–March 1980 the film was shot on location in New York. Its $450,000 cost was underwritten by a group of investors, including London Weekend Television and Polytel, backers previously of *Hullabaloo*.

The movie opens with the auction of the Austen play at Sotheby's in New York, bought by George Midash (Michael Wager), head of a family arts foundation. He has been spurred on in the bidding by

(above) The clergyman, Mr. Foot, snatches his Book of Common Prayer out of the fire, where the kidnapped Miss Byron has tossed it in order to avoid being forcibly married to the villainous Sir Hargrave Pollexfen.

(opposite) The same Jane Austen play being rehearsed for a radically different version: *(standing)* Nancy New and Sean Young; *(living furniture)* Charles McCaughan as a bench, Philip Lenkowsky as Miss Byron's tea table.

Pierre (Robert Powell), who is ambitious to produce the play for his Off-Broadway avant-garde theater group. The radicalism of his approach is quickly seen in episodes that follow, in which his disciples perform in puppet-like roles under his guidance, and traditional texts are deconstructed and then reassembled as Absurdist farce. A number of subplots are introduced, sometimes in flashback, involving the theme of kidnapping or abduction in the Austen play and its counterpart in the rival companies of Pierre and Lilianna Zorska (Anne Baxter), a staunch traditionalist in the theater and Pierre's one-time mentor and lover. A young actress, Ariadne (Sean Young), has been induced to leave her husband Victor (Kurt Johnson), a young star of the Broadway musical stage, by the wily Pierre, who wants her as a member of his commune—which means that she must be under his exclusive control, must cut her ties with everyone except him. Victor then appeals to Lilianna to help him get her back. Charming eighteenth-century enactments of the heroine's abduction in the play are interposed between scenes of Ariadne's "abduction" and the effort to recover her as the action of the film and the play-within-the-film come to mirror each other.

Jane Austen resembles *Hullabaloo Over Georgie and Bonnie's Pic-*

tures specifically, and in some sense grows out of it, since it involves the theme of manipulation and intrigue, the struggle to possess a prized work of art. Lilianna not only assists Victor in attempting to win back Ariadne but also seeks to get the arts foundation grant and produce the Austen work herself as an eighteenth-century opera. She and Pierre are like Clark Haven and Lady Gee as arch rivals, but their motives have deeper roots. Lilianna had been jilted by the younger Pierre, and getting the grant and the play is a way of spiting him. She turns out to be fully as manipulative as Pierre, and more successful. Pierre initially gets the grant and the chance to do the play, but when

Lilianna (Anne Baxter), also with kidnapping in mind, tries to entice Miss Byron/Ariadne (Sean Young) away from the mesmeric Pierre.

Two con artists face each other down. Lilianna with Pierre/Sir Hargrave Pollexfen (Robert Powell).

Ivory with composer Richard Robbins, in the opera house at Cohoes, New York. (1980)

he does produce it and it dismays the foundation committee, he loses both grant and play—as well as most of his actors—to Lilianna.

Although *Jane Austen* is conspicuous for its ensemble acting, Robert Powell and Anne Baxter have the dominant roles. Powell brings a cool, charismatic quality to Pierre, whose commune is curiously like an ashram, in which the young actor-disciples must give absolute devotion to a pure idea he himself embodies. He is a kind of kinsman to Ustad Zafar Khan in *The Guru* and to the other gurus in Jhabvala's fiction. One of the picture's chief pleasures is provided by Baxter's performance as Lilianna, still beautiful in middle age and in full command of her actress's cunning arts that she had demonstrated years earlier as Eve Harrington in *All About Eve*. In an amusing scene late in the film, Midash tells her that as a child (clearly overprotected by his mother), the other boys had kicked over his sand castles; and Lilianna shrewdly wins him over as a mother surrogate, assuring him that she won't let the other boys destroy *his* sand castles. In the end, she "abducts" Pierre's actors and stages the work as an opera. But it is a very harmonious ending: characters turn out to be other than what they had at first seemed, and elements of Pierre's innovative methods are used in the opera, making it both traditional and modern.

The movie's ending involves some sleight of hand, and its complications tend to be labyrinthine. But it is full of delightful things, including Richard Robbins's lively and inventive score for the opera, a Mozartian pastiche. Ernest Vincze's color photography gives *Jane Austen* the look of a film costing many times what it did; and Ivory, along the way, has created an intriguing theatrical subculture in New York. Perhaps the hand most visible in the movie is Jhabvala's, whose screenplay is so textured and "literary" that it is surprising it works. *Jane Austen* is an elegant entertainment.

Isabelle Adjani before a take during the shooting of *Quartet.* (1980)

QUARTET
(1981)

JUST AS JHABVALA had interested Ivory in reading more of Henry James, leading eventually to the making of *The Europeans*, she now introduced him to the novels of Jean Rhys, which led to his decision to film her early work *Quartet*. Part of Ivory's interest in the novel sprang from his own early visit to Paris in 1950, where the sense of the city in the 1920s could still be felt—a Golden Age, although a complicated one, that is recreated in the movie. The film was shot on location in Paris with a largely French crew, and cost $1.8 million to make, with financing coming from Gaumont in Paris, the French government agency Avance sur Recettes, 20th Century Fox in London, and Roger Corman's New World Pictures in Los Angeles.

Rhys's *Quartet* (1928) is an autobiographical novel that came out of her experience in Paris in 1922 when she was in her mid-twenties. She had been born to British parents in the West Indies, where she spent her early years in a convent school; but at sixteen she was sent to live with an aunt in England. For a time she studied at the Royal Academy of Dramatic Art, but when her father died, she was forced to scrape a living as a chorus girl with musical-comedy touring companies, an unhappy and disillusioning experience. In London she met and married a European poet and journalist, and they took up a bohemian life in Paris. The illegal currency dealings in which her husband was involved, however, landed him in jail, and when he was released, he abandoned Rhys suddenly. Without money and in a despondent state, Rhys then met the novelist Ford Madox Ford and his wife, Stella, a painter. When she showed them a novel she was writing,

At Boeuf-sur-le-Toit, Lois Heidler (Maggie Smith) and a confidante (Sheila Gish).

Ford asked her to come to live with them so that he could help her with her work. Before long, however, she found herself not only Ford's protégée but also his mistress—while Stella Ford, who had stoically accepted her husband's infidelities in the past, tried to look the other way. Before long the affair ran its course, and Rhys was in effect ousted when Ford found her a ghostwriting job on the Riviera.

In *Quartet*, Rhys gives her own fictional account of what transpired through her heroine Marya Zelli, who is poor and adrift in Paris. At the center of the novel is Marya's relationship to H. J. Heidler, a thinly disguised version of Ford, in which she is exploited and abandoned. A work of less than two hundred pages, *Quartet* is written in a tight, telegraphic style in which paragraphs may be only a few sentences long; it is flawed in some respects—in its narration that switches back and forth awkwardly between the third and first person, and in its shrill but never fully articulated emotions—but it has a strong psychological interest. Marya is a curious case, very dependent on men, and subject to spells of passivity that come over her powerfully and reduce her to utter helplessness. Her emotional state and sense of betrayal give the novel its special vision of Paris in the 1920s as a setting of exploitation and powerlessness. In London Marya had been repelled by the

English pretense of caring about others; she had expected to find more human warmth in the French, yet discovers that they "pretend every bit as much, only about different things and not so obviously." Nothing in Paris is what it seems, and in the end Marya is overwhelmed by the "unreality of everything."

Jhabvala's screenplay is faithful to the novel in essentials but creates a somewhat different tone and style. Rhys's Montparnasse, where characters like Marya live in cheap hotels, is a sparsely sketched background; but in the movie the sense of place has foreground importance. The comfortably-off Heidlers and others of their circle belong to Paris in the 1920s, to the boulevards and cafés that Hemingway had known and would recall as a "movable feast"; and its period details, handsomely photographed by Pierre Lhomme, are scrupulously authentic. The makeup, hair and clothing styles of the women, the Heidlers' Art Deco apartment, and the Left Bank boite where a black chanteuse (Armelia McQueen) sings a rousing torch song, "Full-time Lover," composed by Richard Robbins, belong to a very specific place and moment.

Lhomme's camera follows Marya closely as her experience in the city—it is a kind of wandering—describes a circle. Her Polish husband Stefan (Anthony Higgins), an illicit dealer in art objects, is arrested one day and sent to prison, leaving her with no means of support. In the meantime, she has attracted the interest of a couple named Heidler—H. J. (Alan Bates), an art patron, and his wife Lois (Maggie Smith), who paints. One day at a restaurant, having learned of her circumstances, Heidler asks her to come to live with them. Reluctantly, but having little choice since she can no longer afford to pay for her hotel room, she accepts the offer. The arrangement gives Heidler the opportunity to indulge his compulsion to take advantage of lost young girls, while keeping up appearances, "playing the game." It is a spider-

(above left) Marya Zelli (Isabelle Adjani) is told to hurry up and get undressed.

(above right) The Pornographer (Pierre Clementi) is roughed up by his models for nonpayment of wages.

(opposite left) A. J. Heidler (Alan Bates), and *(right)* Stefan Zelli (Anthony Higgins).

114

and-fly situation, with Marya the victim. Marya is weak enough to fall in love with Heidler when he seduces her; and Lois is weak enough to permit the affair, being unable to live without the man who dominates her.

But the triangular relationship proves torturing to all involved, and in the end Marya is abandoned by Heidler, and by Stefan, too, after his release from prison. The novel concludes with Marya alone and deserted in Paris, but Jhabvala adds a new ending (she had tried out several) in which Marya is picked up by a man named Schlamovitz, a prison crony of Stefan's, who has just gotten rid of his mistress. As he leads her up a stairway to his apartment, he tells her that he is an "old-fashioned" sort of man. "Nowadays," he remarks, "people live in a dirty way. There is no tradition. There is nothing beautiful." But he is as dubious as Stefan, and the circle is closed with the implication that, as a mere appendage to another man, Marya can find no way out of her marginality and placelessness.

Isabelle Adjani won the Best Actress award at the Cannes Film Festival for her performance as Marya, and she is certainly an extraordinary presence on screen, a "crushed petal type" of exotic beauty, as Lois Heidler describes her. But Adjani's passive waif also creates a problem for the film, since it is very hard to identify with her inner emotions, which, despite a few outbursts, seem screened from the viewer and can only be guessed at. Nor is it easy to believe that she is in love with a man as weak, empty, and easily seen through as H. J. Heidler—a feeling shared by audiences and reviewers. The situation is different with Heidler's wife, Lois, whose desperation is deeply felt in Maggie Smith's superb performance. In one scene Lois falls on her knees before Heidler with barking sobs, and the misery of her marriage registers powerfully.

I disagree. Far from screening her emotions, Adjani's Marya Zelli was always open about them—too open for her own good, once she'd given herself to Heidler and then fallen in love with him. Adjani kept nothing back, veering from a tremulous joy to outbursts of hysterical scorn in the course of her characterization. Of my many heroines stuck on a dubious man, I would consider Marya, as played by Adjani, the most nakedly passionate. JI

But if *Quartet* is imperfect, it is also involving, a chamber piece with a deep mood of malaise and baffled longing. Marya's sense of entrapment, it becomes clear before long, is shared by the other characters. During the central part of the film, Stefan occupies a prison cell, but even when he is free, he feels imprisoned and desperate. The unhappy marriage of H. J. and Lois is also felt as imprisoning, a pretence of a settled, normal relationship. Heidler, who declares that he is "sick" of himself, is sexually aroused by sensitive, astray girls, but only for a time, because he is actually disgusted by sex. Trapped by his sexual compulsion that gives him no satisfaction, he is forced to live with his sense of futility. Alan Bates and Maggie Smith play off each other splendidly as a couple who have furnished their lives elegantly from the outside with art and artistic interests while gnawed by an inner sense of emptiness, and they reflect Montparnasse and its pretenders.

Ivory acknowledges that an influence on *Quartet*, at least in certain places, was John Glassco's *Memoirs of Montparnasse*, an extraordinarily vivid account of what Paris was really like in the twenties. From *Memoirs*, Ivory drew the scene in which a pornographer (Pierre Clementi) arranges to have Marya call at his studio in the belief that he is a legitimate photographer interested in paying her to model for him. The scene she witnesses at the studio is rendered with a straight-faced

(opposite) Marya's American friend Cairn (Wiley Wood) tries to warn her against the predatory Heidler.

(below) The quartet of novel and film.

wittiness: a woman answers the door dressed in the habit of a nun (but is naked from the back), and in the studio itself the photographer takes pictures of a naked man posing with several girls in an enactment of sadomasochistic sex—until the naked man and the photographer fall into wrangling over money. What is disturbing about Montparnasse in the film is the violent disparity between the quarter's gilded surfaces, with its pretensions to sensitivity and emotional refinement, and its underlay of meanness.

Quartet may seem like a departure from other Merchant Ivory films, but it does belong to their world. It contains a number of their themes and is a meditation on a particular culture in a time of change. In earlier films, Ivory's Westerners who come to India discover illusion and the distance between themselves and others; and something similar happens in *Quartet* when its rootless foreigners come to Paris in search of greater fulfillment in its aesthetic surroundings. Here style and the observance of outward forms are all-important, even though in the period following World War I the values presumed to stand behind them have collapsed. Soon the outsiders become involved in "playing the game" by French rules, as they attempt to deal with the formless-ness of their own lives and the sense of futility they feel. Involved in a Parisian charade in which an elation in living and in the arts goes hand in hand with despair, they cannot become "real," achieve any solid identity. *Quartet* did not fare well with audiences, which found it "unwholesome," but it is a distinctive film with an interest that is to a large extent psychological. It is also a sustained poetic evocation of one of Ivory's most frequently recurring themes—the longing for an ideal that remains poignantly out of reach.

THE COURTESANS OF BOMBAY
(1983)

AFTER COMPLETING *QUARTET*, Merchant and Ivory
returned to India, where they prepared two movies during
1981–82. The more modestly scaled, and the first to be
released (in January 1983), was the 73-minute documentary (or "docu-
drama," as Merchant refers to it) *The Courtesans of Bombay*, which was
both produced and directed by Merchant. Merchant first knew of the
courtesans at an early age, he told me, "from the visits from them we
used to have during weddings at home, celebrations of childbirth, and
other festivities. They provided the entertainment of singing and dancing, and I used to watch them." Then at the age of sixteen he was
taken by school friends to Pavan Pool, an enclosed area of Bombay
where the courtesans performed before a male audience, an experience
that remained vividly in his memory and that he now wished to record
on film.

The Courtesans, which cost £100,000 to make, was chiefly financed
by and was first shown on London's Channel 4 television. Its subject,
Pavan Pool, is a small enclave within the city, yet it is a world unto
itself. Four to five thousand people live in its tenements, with as many
as twelve to a room, and a spillover of others live on the stairways and

(opposite) Preparing for their lives as entertainers in Pavan Pool.

(below) The girls wait for their evening to begin.

roofs. Whole families live there, but the breadwinners of Pavan Pool are women who from an early age perform the traditional arts of song and dance in the buildings' beehive of rooms, where male loungers reward their performances with applause and money. Sometimes more is exchanged for rupees than the witnessing of a dance, but *The Courtesans* is very discreet, and the buying of sexual favors, while acknowledged, is not given a prominent place in the film.

An enlivening variety is added by the presence of the movie's three commentators, who also help to put things in focus. The first is the rent collector (Kareem Samar), a bribable, pleasant fellow. Another is a worndown actor in Bombay films (Saeed Jaffrey), who neglects his family to come to Pavan Pool and be entranced by his favorite dancer. The third commentator, played with scene-stealing good nature by Zohra Segal, is a stout, older woman, a retired courtesan who prepares a jar of her famous lime pickles while she explains the customs of Pavan Pool. Dialogue for the three, supplied by Jhabvala, creates a social drama within the otherwise strictly factual documentary, which focuses particularly on the singers and dancers, from girlhood and beyond. The arts they practice have been handed down not only for generations but even for centuries; lately, however, there have been some changes. Disco music has influenced the dancing of the younger and most popular girls who dream, unrealistically, that a producer will appear one day with a film contract. The film opens a window on an exotic and very special world, yet is recognizably a Merchant Ivory film concerned with tradition and change, reality and illusion, in Indian society. It has, too, keen observation and humor, affection and detachment.

Merchant instructs Zohra Segal, one of the actor-narrators of *The Courtesans of Bombay*. (1981)

HEAT AND DUST
(1983)

IT WAS MERCHANT who was the initiator and prime mover in the making of *Heat and Dust*. Jhabvala and Ivory wondered if it would not be going over familiar ground, but he insisted that the release of a new Indian feature film was essential to mark the company's twenty-first-anniversary year. He set the wheels in motion, securing backing from the Rank organization, Roger Wingate of Curzon Film Distributors in London (which had had record-breaking success with *The Europeans*), London's Channel 4 television, and a number of other sources. In all, the film's budget came to $2.2 million. But as had happened in the past, Merchant Ivory walked a financial tightrope. As Merchant remarks: "Halfway through the shooting some of the finance committed to the project failed to materialize, and we found we were suddenly penniless. The cast and crew continued to work despite the fact that they weren't being paid, but that couldn't go on indefinitely. There was the strongest probability that we would go under. We would lose not just the film, but our whole company." Yet in an eleventh-hour drama, Michael White, a friend and well-wisher who had heard of their situation, introduced Merchant to Sir Jacob Rothschild, a member of the prominent European banking family. When Rothschild saw the film, he responded with great enthusiasm and invested the money needed to complete it and bail out Merchant Ivory.

I wanted *Heat and Dust* not only to celebrate our twenty-one years together, but to unite all three of us again in India, as *The Householder* had—but with a much larger theme this time, and I hoped, with much more money. Ruth wrote the screenplay, and as usual, I submitted it to all the Hollywood studios, who politely—and not so politely—declined. One executive wrote, saying, "We are returning Ruth Jhabvala's *Eat My Dust*." We knew we must find our financing in Europe.

Roger Wingate, a distributor, financier, and real-estate developer, as well as the owner of the Curzon Cinema in London, where *The Europeans* had been a long-running success, put up the money for script development. Fred Turner of the Rank organization, who also had blocked rupees in India, liked *Heat and Dust*, as did Jeremy Isaacs and David Rose at Britain's TV Channel Four, which had begun partially to finance low-budget features, and to whom we now sold the television rights to some of our earlier films in order to raise money. Funds were promised by private backers in India, who then unex-

(opposite) 1923: Waiting to be presented at the Nawab of Khatm's durbar.

(above) 1923: Well hidden from view, the purdah ladies eye their English counterparts critically. The most critical of all is the Nawab's mother (Madhur Jaffrey, center, smoking).

pectedly withdrew—vanished into thin air, left for Hong Kong, etc.—at the last minute, or even *after* the last minute. We could not well abandon the project, however. Julie Christie, who plays Anne in the modern sections of the film, had turned down a lucrative offer to star opposite Paul Newman in *The Verdict* in favor of *Heat and Dust*. We had to go forward and just hope that the money to complete it would be found later. Our hard currency came in dribs and drabs, more rupees were scrounged once Rank's had been used up, the English crew lived on promises, but the film inched toward completion. That is always the goal: to finish principal photography. If you can just do that, in time everything else will somehow fall into place. IM

Adapted for the screen by Jhabvala from her Booker prize-winning novel, *Heat and Dust* has an unusually rich background and is closely and intimately related to her previous fiction and screen work. While writing the screenplay of *Autobiography of a Princess*, Jhabvala was also planning her novel *Heat and Dust*, and she used *Autobiography* as a kind of workshop of ideas and themes for the fictional work. As *Autobiography* passed into fiction, its dual time planes—India of the Raj in the 1920s versus a cramped, pedestrian present—became the chief structuring device of the novel. In *Autobiography* the princess and Cyril Sahib are survivors of the earlier time who look back to it with fascination, particularly to the figure of the Maharaja, who had influenced their lives profoundly. In the novel the Nawab of Khatm takes the place of the Maharaja, and a fascination with the Indian past is transferred to the novel's narrator, a modern-day English girl who travels to India, where the past and present are continually evoked and contrasted.

The evolution of *Autobiography* into the novel *Heat and Dust* is complicated by the sense one has of E. M. Forster in the background. In *A Passage to India* Forster laid out indelibly the situation of the English in India and the cultural factors dividing them from the country's natives; and *Heat and Dust* is also concerned with the problem of establishing contact between the two peoples. But Forster was influential more particularly on Jhabvala's conception of two of her characters, the Nawab and his English court companion Harry. Forster had himself had a privileged relationship to a Maharaja, had been a secretary to one, and so for that matter had his young friend J. R. Ackerley who, like himself, was homosexual. Both wrote memoirs about their experience at the courts of these Maharajas that, Ivory acknowledges, provided "wonderful background for *Heat and Dust, Autobiography, Hullabaloo,* and even *Shakespeare Wallah.*" Ackerley's *Hindoo Holiday* (1932) is an account of his experience as private secretary to the (fictional) Maharaja of Chhatarpur; while Forster's *The Hill of Devi* (1953) recounts, in the form of journals and letters home to his mother in England, a brief visit to India in 1912–13 and a longer stay in 1921 when he was private secretary to the Maharaja of Dewas Senior, a small nation-state in central India. Forster's portrait of the Maharaja in *The Hill of Devi* appears particularly to have inspired Jhabvala's Nawab and his court entourage. But Forster himself, or Forster and Ackerley together, provide the idea of Harry in *Heat and Dust,* the English homosexual friend at the court of the Nawab of Khatm. The English secretary figure appears first in *Autobiography* as Cyril Sahib, the Maharaja's tutor, so-called; but he is a trial run for Harry who, living on into old age, is a connecting link between the Indian past and present.

The translation of *Heat and Dust* onto the screen completes a cycle that moves from one art form to another and back—from the film *Autobiography* to the novel *Heat and Dust* and back to *Heat and Dust* as a movie. The cinematic technique of the novel that Jhabvala learned from her film work—the splicing and juxtaposing of scenes, flashbacks and flashforwards—are used again in the medium from which they came to connect past and present. The film tells two stories in parallel, one set in India in the romantic 1920s, and another in the 1970s. In the first, Olivia (Greta Scacchi), a junior administrator's wife, has an affair with the local Nawab (Shashi Kapoor) that shocks the British community, and at the end she goes to live alone in a mountain retreat. The

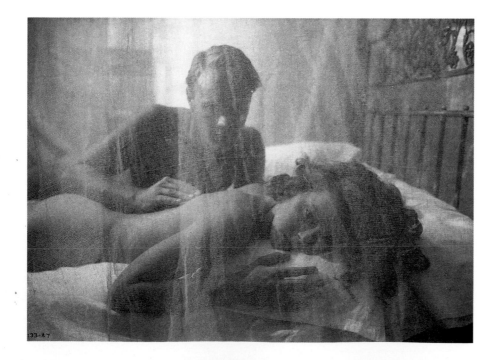

1923: Douglas and Olivia Rivers (Christopher Cazenove and Greta Scacchi).

1923: Harry (Nickolas Grace), the Nawab's friend and long-time guest, comes to tell Olivia that she has caught the Nawab's eye.

second involves her great niece Anne (Julie Christie), who comes to India to research Olivia's life and on a different scale repeats her experience, becoming pregnant by the Indian Inder Lal (Zakir Hussain) and traveling finally to the retreat in the mountains where Olivia had ended her days and where she herself hopes to bear her child.

The film cuts skillfully back and forth between the two stories so that what is common, as well as what is different, in the two heroines' experience is always kept before the viewer. The different time planes and stories have a cohesiveness, too, through a parallelism in certain other characters. The romantic Nawab, as the lover of Olivia, is contrasted with Anne's lover, Inder Lal, a small cog in a large governmental bureaucracy that represents the new India. Harry in the 1920s story, who becomes oppressed by India, falls ill, and wants to go home to England, is played off against the present-day "Chid," an American would-be Hindu whose health is so damaged by the Indian diet and climate that he returns home pathetically to the Midwest at the end.

For her screenplay Jhabvala received both Britain's National Film Critics Award and the British Academy of Film and Television Arts Award for Best Screenplay. In an important sense, it is a summing up of Jhabvala's previous writing about India in both her fiction and screenwriting. Her earlier Maharajas, English colonials, and English girls who form relationships with Indian men and sometimes, in the enigma of India, go over the edge into the "unknown" are all incorporated into the movie. The members of the English colony are themselves a study, and Ivory has captured them with a quiet perfection of inflection. Major Minnies (Barry Foster), the Crawfords (Julian Glover and Susan Fleetwood), and Dr. Saunders and his wife (Patrick Godfrey and Jennifer Kendal) are all longtime residents in the country and know where the lines are drawn between themselves and the Indians. Major

(left) 1923: No Merchant Ivory film is said to be complete without a big dinner party, and this is the biggest of them all: the Nawab and his guests toast the King-Emperor, George V.

(above) 1980: Chid (Charles McCaughan), the American *sanyasi* and would-be Hindu holy man.

(below) 1923: The Nawab and his friends play musical cushions.

1923: In India the ancient caste of men who dress and act like women are called *hijra*, or sometimes "eunuchs." We would call them "transvestites," or perhaps "cross-dressers." (Traditionally, they make their living by ribald singing and dancing when the birth of a baby boy is being celebrated.) In this scene from *Heat and Dust*, the Nawab, as a joke, has summoned them to entertain his foreign friends.

Minnies can appreciate Indian art, and he stays on in the Subcontinent after his retirement, but he stands apart from what he calls "the other dimension of life in India." There is never any doubt that the Crawfords will ever step beyond the Civil Lines; they are too practical for that, and as Harry tells Olivia, too "dull." Of all the members of the British colony, Dr. Saunders and his morbid wife are surely the most unattractive. The heat and dust of India have worked on them for so long that they seem at the point of constant exasperation. Dr. Saunders possesses a grim, vengeful moralism that is repelling, and his wife projects lustful fantasies upon her Indian servants, warning Olivia that all they think about "is to do you know what with a white woman."

Throughout the 1920s story, distrust and resentment exist between the English and the Indians, with Olivia, who is sensitive to the country's attractions—to the "other dimension"—caught between the two groups. The Italian-born English actress Greta Scacchi was extraordinarily well cast as Olivia because, although very much a well-bred English girl, she has a certain Mediterranean bloom about her. She responds to music and art, and Harry calls her living room an "oasis," where personal relationships can be fostered. But just because she is sensitive, she becomes drawn to the Nawab, a sensitive or imaginative man. In certain scenes, like the elaborate dinner party he gives, he seems like an Indian Gatsby. But just as the English intrigue against the Nawab, reducing him ultimately from a ruler to a pawn, he intrigues against them; and his affair with Olivia is partly manipulative. When she becomes pregnant, presumably by the Nawab, he is overjoyed as he thinks of the smart it will give to his English oppressors. The pregnancy gives a smart most of all, however, to Olivia, who, rather than risk the chance that the child she is carrying is the Nawab's, has it aborted.

The modern story of Anne seems bland compared to the 1920s one, although deliberately so, because it is a more subdued world. The Anglo-Indian tensions have lessened in post-Empire India, yet the mys-

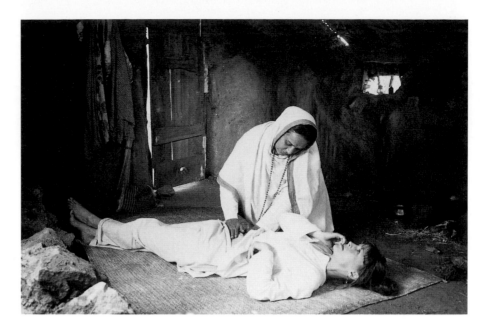

1980: Anne (Julie Christie) suddenly decides against having an abortion.

tery of the country persists, and Anne, too, is drawn to the mountains, to isolation and inwardness. What is notable about *Heat and Dust* is that, rather than surging with strong outward passions, it focuses upon the increasing inwardness of its dual heroines. The refined observation and quiet lyricism of the film are enhanced considerably by Walter Lassally's camera work, which captures the Indian scene and landscape in ravishing images so that India itself becomes the most important "character" in the movie.

The presence of India is also evoked effectively in the score by Richard Robbins, who had by then already been initiated into Indian music. He had been drawn to it originally when he was living in Europe and discovered the films of Satyajit Ray. He was so moved by the music Ray composed for his films that he began to take an interest in Indian music more generally. Then, after making *Sweet Sounds* with Merchant Ivory, he traveled with Merchant to the Punjab, where they enjoyed three days and nights (the star performers often don't begin to play until as late as three or four in the morning) of classical Indian music. The evocation of India in the music of *Heat and Dust*, Robbins told me, comes importantly from the flute sound. "We had a wonderful maestro in Pandit Chaurasia," he said, "who is probably the premier flute player in the world. In fact, we had three notable maestros— Chaurasia, Zakir Hussain, the great tabla player, and Sultan Khan, the famous sarangai player. We had many, many recording sessions in a studio in London." Robbins's score manages to suggest in its themes not only the cultural conflict and sometimes the interrelatedness of East and West but also both the 1920s and the contemporary period— differences within the Indian world conveyed by different kinds of Indian music. *Heat and Dust* was also the first film in which Robbins used synthesizers in composing his scores, combining them here with Indian instruments so that they help to create a sustained mood and quietly lyrical involvement with the country.

The quality of the ensemble acting in *Heat and Dust* is impeccable: Nickolas Grace, for example, as the Nawab's English court companion, and Christopher Cazenove, as Olivia's decent but unimaginative husband, Douglas, have a naturalness in key with the naturalness of the direction. But the film belongs to Greta Scacchi—an unknown, twenty-two-year-old beauty only a year out of drama school who was cast as Olivia just as production was about to begin. The film made her a star. It was also, by chance, perfectly timed, coming at the beginning of a new wave of interest in India in the cinema. *Gandhi* (1982) appeared first, quickly followed by *Heat and Dust* (1983), David Lean's *A Passage to India* (1983), the fourteen-part television series "The Jewel in the Crown" (1983), and the eight-part television series "The Far Pavilions" (1983–1984). An international film audience suddenly awakened to films about India that Merchant Ivory had pioneered.

Heat and Dust was Merchant Ivory's biggest commercial success to date. Its chances were harmed in the U.S. when its distributor, Universal Classics, underwent a change of management that brought things to a standstill virtually on the day it opened. But it was a huge success everywhere else, particularly in England. It marked a turning point for the company, a period film on a large scale that presaged Merchant Ivory's big period film successes that loomed just on the horizon.

(above) 1923: The Nawab (Shashi Kapoor).

(below) 1980: Anne and Chid.

128

CHAPTER VI

The Mid-Eighties—
James and Forster

THE BOSTONIANS
(1984)

IVORY RECALLS THAT it "was in 1972 or so that I got on this Henry James kick and began to read everything." He liked *The Bostonians* and could envision it as a film, but he did not consider it seriously until almost a decade later. In 1980, as it happened, WGBH television in Boston drew up plans for a five-part series on the James family, with four hour-long profiles each of Henry James, senior, and his famous offspring William, Henry, and Alice. The fifth segment was to be a dramatization of a work by Henry James, which the station asked Merchant Ivory to do, choosing the work themselves. The work Ivory chose was *The Bostonians*. WGBH applied for funding to the National Endowment for the Humanities, and Jhabvala went ahead with a screen version of the novel. In 1981, however, the Reagan administration slashed the NEH's budget, and the five-part series had to be abandoned. But by then Jhabvala had written her screenplay, and in 1983 Merchant Ivory made the decision to shoot it as a feature film. Merchant secured financing for the $3 million project chiefly from Rediffusion, Curzon Film Distributors, Almi (the film's American distributor), and the Rank organization.

The casting of Vanessa Redgrave in the key role of Olive Chancellor has an interesting and piquant background. Redgrave had been Merchant Ivory's first choice for Eugenia in *The Europeans* and for Lois Heidler in *Quartet,* but she had other commitments and the roles went

(opposite) Basil Ransom (Christopher Reeve) and Olive Chancellor (Vanessa Redgrave) take each other's measure at the beginning of their war for Verena Tarrant.

(above) Basil Ransom woos a reluctant Verena (Madeleine Potter) in Central Park.

to other stars. In casting Olive, their first choice was again Redgrave, but she turned down the role, then told Merchant Ivory that she was very interested in doing it when Glenn Close had already accepted the part and had even been fitted for her costumes in London. Not long before shooting was due to begin, however, Barry Levinson decided that he wanted Close for his film *The Natural*, which was to be made in Buffalo at about the same time as *The Bostonians* was to be shot. Close's agent then informed Merchant that he would have to arrange her schedule to accommodate Levinson's film, and he eventually demanded that Merchant Ivory release her from their set whenever it was necessary for her to go to Buffalo—an arrangement that would have made the production cost of the tightly scheduled *Bostonians* prohibitive. At this point, Merchant let Close out and signed Redgrave for the part of Olive Chancellor.

The making of *The Bostonians* came at a particularly difficult time in Redgrave's career, as Ivory relates in his article "The Trouble with Olive," in the spring 1985 issue of *Sight and Sound*. "In April 1982," Ivory writes, "Vanessa Redgrave was in effect fired by the Boston Symphony Orchestra without notice when a series of performances of *Oedipus Rex* at Symphony Hall in Boston and Carnegie Hall in New York was cancelled. She had been engaged to narrate the Stravinsky work. No official version was given for the Symphony's action, but it was widely suspected that her sympathies for the PLO made her unacceptable to the Symphony's Jewish trustees and fund raisers. There had been unsubstantiated rumors of threats of uproar and violence by the Jewish Defense League if she were allowed to perform, and the Symphony management was thought to have panicked, justifying their

Doctor Prance (Linda Hunt) fraternally wishes her friend Basil Ransom luck in Marmion.

action on the grounds of public safety. News of all this—or just bad rumors—had a sort of domino effect in New York, and she lost a Broadway part because of the cancellation. For fourteen months after that she did no work." Redgrave filed a lawsuit against the orchestra that bitterly divided the Boston arts community; the suit was widely publicized in the press and was still in litigation when *The Bostonians* went into production. It was in Boston, the setting of all this controversy, that Redgrave prepared the role of Olive—a woman, like herself, with political views.

James's *The Bostonians*, which deals with feminists and reformers in Boston after the Civil War, is dramatic in structure and many of its confrontational scenes, yet would seem impossible to transfer to the stage or screen. Its story concerns a strenuous Back Bay spinster (Olive Chancellor) of high-strung nerves and unconscious lesbianism, who adopts a vibrant young inspirational speaker (Verena Tarrant) as her companion in the Woman's Movement, only to have her wooed away by the Southerner Basil Ransom, an intransigent reactionary and male chauvinist who is in his way as unattractive as she. Considering especially the difficulties she faced (the eccentricity of the material and the lack of many sympathetic characters), Jhabvala's screenplay is remarkable. It is faithful to the original in many respects but not wholly (Jhabvala creates an entirely new ending); it mutes James's piercing and at times exuberant satire for the sake of plausible period realism; and it gives to Olive—to whom James shows no mercy—understanding and sympathy. Ivory's pictures have previously contained outsider characters, but Olive, as played by Redgrave, is the "great" outsider, whose struggle to come to terms with her nature is the energy of the film.

As in *The Europeans*, their earlier adaptation of James, Ivory makes very effective use of the scenic arts, creating a New England that is both accurate in historical details and extremely evocative. Walter Lassally's camera lovingly captures Boston and Cambridge, Harvard Yard, New York's Central Park, and the luminous landscapes and seascapes of Martha's Vineyard, standing in for Cape Cod. The musical score by Richard Robbins also enriches the work, heightening and commenting on its various moods. Robbins's music enters effectively into a number of scenes. One occurs when Verena and Basil visit Harvard's Memorial Hall, commemorating the university's students who had given their lives in the Civil War. In the novel the scene is intended to suggest the idea of ennobling sacrifice transcending the rancor of ideological differences. The lofty and affirmative music Robbins selected for the sequence was Brahms's Alto Rhapsody, which, in fact, had its American premiere in Boston just at the time when the film is set. The problem of how to introduce it was solved by Robbins in a most ingenious way—by creating the impression that the Brahms piece (with its piano, men's chorus, and contralto soloist) was in rehearsal and could be heard distinctly from an adjacent auditorium just as Verena and Basil were visiting Memorial Hall.

The film contains many fine, highly styled moments: Olive and

Dr. Tarrant (Wesley Addy) "starts up" Verena. Mrs. Tarrant (Barbara Bryne) and Mr. Pardon (Wallace Shawn) look on.

(overleaf) Olive searches the sea off Cape Cod for the missing Verena; *(inset)* Vanessa Redgrave and Madeleine Potter.

133

Miss Birdseye (Jessica Tandy) on the beach.

Verena, wearing long white dresses as they dance together by the seashore in a lyric moment that is also a lament; Miss Birdseye (Jessica Tandy), aged and near death, as she sits alone under a beach umbrella in the hot Cape Cod sun, her face bleached of expression. It also incorporates moments of Jamesian humor and some of his drawing-room scenes, including the dramatic one at Mrs. Burrage's home in New York, where Olive jousts with Mrs. Burrage, a society matron played suavely by Nancy Marchand.

As Verena, Madeleine Potter in her first film appearance is at least partially successful. She lacks authority as a public speaker who can hold and enchant audiences, but she is plausible as a susceptible girl torn between her love for Olive and for Basil; she brings passion to this aspect of the role, and touching shades of innocence, though she is intentionally overshadowed by Redgrave and Reeve. Christopher Reeve is striking as Basil Ransom, and all the more so because of his then recent celebrity as Superman, which brought him fame but seemed to deny him stature as a serious actor. What is especially good about Reeve is how wonderfully persuasive he is, the way he brings an almost mesmeric concentration to the role. In skillfully lit close-ups of his face, his prominent eyes and handsome features can be startling and are used by him as weapons in his single-minded effort to win Verena.

The Bostonians is conspicuous for its ensemble acting. Redgrave, Reeve, and Potter are locked into an intense triangular relationship, of which one never ceases to be conscious, even in confrontational scenes in which one of the three is absent. Nevertheless, the great role is Redgrave's. It is a towering performance—winning her an Academy Award nomination as Best Actress—that captures Olive's vulnerability and her strength. With her wire-rimmed spectacles and tense demeanor, Redgrave has the appearance of an angular spinster who stands outside the main currents of her society. Yet she becomes impressive in her suffering. Ivory employs skillful close-ups of her care-worn face—sometimes as she stands by a window lost in thought or as she is distraught on the beach—that emphasize her isolation and inner suffering. Redgrave plays Olive with tremendous conviction, inhabits the role fully, and brings to James's chilly spinster a remarkable warmth. Jhabvala's magnanimous conception of Olive is seen particularly at the end where Olive appears before the angry crowd at the Boston Music Hall not to be destroyed, as in the novel, but to be reborn.

The Bostonians is less distanced from its central characters than some of Ivory's previous films, which probably contributed to its enthusiastic reception. In an admiring review, *The New York Times* remarked that Merchant, Ivory, and Jhabvala "have not only endured as collaborators but, it's now apparent, they have enriched and refined their individual talents to the point where they have made what must be one of their best films as well as one of the best adaptations of a major literary work ever to come onto the screen." *The Bostonians* also enjoyed success at the box office, having such explosive sales in its first week at Cinema I in New York that it was soon being screened at thirty movie houses in the metropolitan area, and at nearly two hundred others across the country where Merchant Ivory's films had rarely been shown.

The worldly Mrs. Burrage (Nancy Marchand) gives Olive Chancellor some unwelcome advice.

A ROOM WITH A VIEW
(1986)

ALTHOUGH E. M. FORSTER has special importance for Jhabvala in his depiction of the English in India that affords a multiplicity of perspectives, it was Ivory who proposed the adaptation of his novel *A Room with a View*. "In 1980," he remarks, "I initiated *A Room with a View* and Ismail and Ruth were swept along. Time passed. We made *Heat and Dust* and *The Bostonians*, and I said: 'I can't do another period picture. I can't do another literary adaptation.' But we had been paid for the script, so the other two told me, 'Just get on with it!'" In the end, Ivory found making *A Room with a View* "enormously enjoyable" because it was "lighter and more frivolous" than his usual movies. Merchant obtained financial backing for the $3 million production from Cinecom in the U.S., and from Goldcrest Films, the National Film Finance Corporation, and Curzon Film Distributors in Great Britain. The movie was shot on location in Florence, where Merchant Ivory had the Piazza della Signoria cleared

(above) The Emersons charm the Misses Alan in the Pensione Bertolini: *(left to right)* Denholm Elliott, Fabia Drake, Julian Sands, Joan Henley.

(opposite) In Fiesole, *(left to right)* Eleanor Lavish (Judy Dench), Charlotte Bartlett (Maggie Smith), and Lucy Honeychurch (Helena Bonham Carter).

Lighter and more frivolous to be sure, but there was another reason I wanted to make *A Room With a View:* I felt it was time to revisit Italy after a twenty-year absence, and *A Room With a View* gave me an excuse to do that. Many people thought it was strange that Merchant

Ivory had no interest in *A Passage to India* and would ask me why, when Forster's executors at Cambridge had proposed our filming what is generally considered to be his finest work, we had turned it down. In fact, the book's fame was one of the main reasons against doing it. We felt we'd be the targets for all sorts of brickbats. In the early 1980s we could no longer count on the kind of enthusiastic critical reception we'd often enjoyed in the 1960s and only sometimes in the 1970s. But there was another, and a better, reason for us to decline; Satyajit Ray very much wanted to film *A Passage to India* and had even visited Forster in England in order to persuade him to give him the rights, arranging for the *Apu Trilogy* to be shown to him. But Forster stubbornly resisted letting any of his books be made into films, and Ray was rebuffed. The prohibition did not extend to the stage or to television; the author Santa Rama Rao had done very well-received adaptations of *A Passage to India* in both

for filming, and in England, where they borrowed the Kent family estate of film critic John Pym for their country scenes. In all, it was shot in ten weeks.

Although it lacks the complexity and breadth of *Howards End* and *A Passage to India*, *A Room with a View* is one of Forster's most delightful and immediately engaging novels. A witty comedy of Edwardian manners, it moves swiftly and dramatically, lending itself readily to Jhabvala's screen adaptation, to which Ivory also contributed. As Ivory explains: "Ruth wrote her version, and I didn't like it, and nothing happened to it for about a year. I went out to Oregon and rewrote it, put in a lot of stuff that I wanted to have in it. And she then saw it and felt that I had gone too far in certain directions. But she liked some of the things I had done, and she then took her version and my version, and came up with a new version."

Like the novel, the movie has a relatively uncomplicated narrative. In 1907 a young English girl, Lucy Honeychurch, and her spinster cousin, Charlotte Bartlett, stay at the Pensione Bertolini while vacationing in Florence; and there, among other English guests, meet the freethinking Mr. Emerson and his handsome, unhappy son, George.

After the women find that their rooms do not have a view, an exchange of rooms (most "indelicate" Charlotte thinks) is made with the Emersons. From this point on, complications arise, and when George kisses Lucy passionately in the Florentine hills, Charlotte becomes alarmed and cuts short their visit. Back in England, Lucy becomes engaged to the priggish Cecil Vyse; but when the Emersons turn up in their English village, she begins to discover who she is. As basic human needs triumph joyfully over convention, Lucy rejects Cecil for George, the vital man, and the two appear at the end on their honeymoon amid the aesthetic and sensual surroundings of Florence. *A Room with a View* is Ivory's sunniest and most confident comedy of manners.

The Edwardian setting and the natural scenery of Italy in *A Room with a View* were photographed sumptuously by Tony Pierce-Roberts, and its romantic themes are richly evoked in the music of Richard Robbins and in his selection of arias from Puccini's *Gianni Schicchi* and *La Rondine*, sung by Kiri Te Kanawa. As it happened, Robbins's choice of Puccini, with his direct romantic appeal, was unplanned at the beginning. He remembers that when the first cut of the film was screened, Jhabvala felt that something was lacking in it; the music that Robbins was now to provide, she felt, should include romantic arias from begin-

mediums. However, once Forster had died and his executors had decided to lift the ban, it seems Ray was no longer as keen to make the film for a number of reasons. So I felt it was awkward to attempt to do it myself at that point. JI

(opposite) Helena Bonham Carter and Julian Sands.

(opposite below) Lucy Honeychurch at the piano with her brother Freddy (Rupert Graves).

(right) Cecil Vyse (Daniel Day Lewis) asks Lucy Honeychurch to be his wife.

(overleaf, left) George Emerson and Freddy Honeychurch douse the Reverend Mr. Beebe (Simon Callow) at the Sacred Lake.

(overleaf, right) Finding the exact change so Cousin Charlotte can tip her driver.

I felt—still feel—the lack of any operatic aria by a male singer in the film. I don't know where we would have put it, however, and its exclusion was not from a lack of trying to find the right spot or the right aria. But we had no more room in the Florentine section and never seriously tried putting such an aria into the English half, where it might have been made to work very well. Who knows? JI

ning to end. It didn't seem to him that the film could have arias throughout, since a different, more restrained kind of music would be necessary in the second, or English, half; but he did decide to use arias prominently in Florence, first at the beginning to establish the Italian atmosphere immediately, and then at the moment of the kiss between George Emerson and Lucy in the barley field.

As yet he had not decided exactly what arias to use, but one afternoon he called on his friend Dorle Soria, prominent in the music world in New York and a great connoisseur of opera, and they listened to records for hours. "Although I knew the *Gianni Schicchi* aria very well," Robbins remarked, "I hadn't thought about it in this context, and when Dorle played it, it suddenly seemed absolutely right. I knew several recordings of it but had never heard Kiri Te Kanawa's until that afternoon. Her performance was stunning, it was like an entirely new piece to me." The Puccini arias, which were not then well known to the general public but have often been sung in concert since *A Room with a View* appeared, are one of the great features of the film. They call up immediately the richness of its setting and romantic atmosphere, but their inclusion came about in large part serendipitously.

Certain other musical passages in *A Room with a View* were carefully prepared from the beginning. In earlier Merchant Ivory films, a young woman of good, often middle-class family plays the piano at some point. Eugenia plays the Clara Schumann Trio in *The Europeans* and Olivia plays the piano in *Heat and Dust*; but Lucy in *A Room with a View* does not merely play the piano but is imputed by Forster to be a talented pianist. Her playing, indeed, is meant to suggest the spark of romantic emotion in her nature that will be kindled into rebellion when she chooses at the end to marry George.

141

"I wanted to make a very special case for her," Robbins told me, "as being convincingly a superior pianist, and I persuaded Jim and Ismail that in order to make that impression we didn't want to take the camera from her hands. She is supposed to play very difficult Beethoven, and I rehearsed this passage with Helena Bonham Carter for at least an hour a day all the while we were shooting in Florence. I played the passage on tape and coached Helena in the movement of her body, her shoulders, and the placement of her fingers on the keyboard in the right place at the right time in a convincing way. Then later in London she plays a Schubert piece, and we were careful to show her hands there, too. Many people, including a number of pianists, were convinced that she was playing."

Every aspect of the production of *A Room* was executed with the utmost care and polish, but the movie's success comes chiefly from its superlative cast, and the ensemble acting Ivory draws from them. Maggie Smith is marvelously spinsterish—prim, well meaning, and anxious—but she is not a caricature. Her hollow eyes betray the human price she has paid for being inoffensive; and if she is at times comic, she is also touching. Two older spinster sisters, Catherine Alan (Fabia Drake) and Teresa Alan (Joan Henley), are also touching in their humanity and have great charm. Denholm Elliott, an accomplished actor, brings warmth to Mr. Emerson, socially bumbling but with a strong heart and belief in mankind; and it is surprising how much emotional fullness Julian Sands as George brings to what might have been a stock role. Actually, almost all of the actors are sympathetic— Simon Callow, for instance, as the exuberantly good-natured, bicycle-riding, and cigarette-smoking Reverend Beebe; and all the Honeychurches: Rosemary Leach as the mother, Helena Bonham Carter as the beautiful young Lucy, and Rupert Graves as her coltish brother Freddy.

A Room contains elements of satire that can be seen in its wryest form in the Reverend Eager (Patrick Godfrey), whose serious demeanor throws a damper on any form of pleasure or spontaneity; and in its most exuberant in Daniel Day Lewis's portrayal of Cecil Vyse, a young man belonging more to bookish connoisseurship than to actual living. Lewis is an actor of exceptional versatility (*My Beautiful Launderette*, in which he plays an ingratiating London punk at the furthest remove from Cecil, opened in New York on the same day as *A Room*), and his interpretation of Cecil is idiosyncratic and inspired. It is partly spirited caricature yet also makes Cecil believable as a vulnerable, easily wounded young man. Cecil appears in the central scene at the Sacred Lake, as he leads Mrs. Honeychurch and Lucy through a glade and they come onto George, Freddy, and the Reverend Beebe in the nude, disporting themselves wildly in and around the water. In this scene, which one critic called "an explosion of movement and light and physical joy that is one of the great things in recent movies," satire and the motif of liberation from the constraints of society meet and merge.

(below) Lucy and her fiancé stumble across Freddy in the bracken.

(opposite, left) Mr. Emerson (Denholm Elliott), and *(right)* The fumbled kiss.

In a 1973 article in the British film magazine *Sight and Sound*, John Gillett described Jim and me as "two resilient, international optimists who continue to plan and organize in the belief that the best is yet to come. Ivory suggests, half jokingly, that Merchant is bound some day to have a really big financial success, 'either from me or, I suspect, from someone else.' Anything less would seem a betrayal of destiny."

This prophecy came true with the success of *A Room With a View*, which indeed was a blockbuster. After this success, we were flooded with dozens of proposals from Wall Street to go public. They wanted us to be paid huge salaries, to change our offices, be seen at the right parties, hobnob with the rich and mighty, and court Hollywood executives. Scripts kept arriving from the studios, with big stars attached and huge budgets to pay them with. But for the most part, the scripts were shallow and had been endlessly revised by several different writers. This was not how we saw ourselves. None of it had any link to our methods of moviemaking. And we didn't want to become the flavor of the month. When we took up *An Innocent Millionaire* in 1986, I felt a budget of between $7 to $8 million—twice the amount we'd ever had—should be sufficient, but United Artists was thinking of $17 million—not a Merchant Ivory movie. IM

The movie was greeted by glowing reviews and enjoyed a popular success on a scale unexpected by Merchant Ivory and unprecedented in their experience. *A Room* drew a record-setting $1 million in ticket sales in its first fifteen weeks at the Paris Theatre in New York before being shown across the country. In all, it grossed $24 million in the U.S. and Canada alone, and over $60 million worldwide—amazing figures for an art film. In my interview with her, I asked film historian Annette Insdorf why she thought *A Room* had such an impact on movie audiences. The film, she told me, "has a delicacy, a charm, a whimsical quality, and an intelligence that audiences had been starved for. It strips away the social veneer of the characters and reveals basic human needs and their impulses, and there is something refreshing and liberating about that. But I wouldn't describe the movie as being merely timely. Merchant Ivory films seem to have an atemporal relationship to other films being made at the same time; *A Room with a View* feels as if it could have been made at any time in film history. It has a timeless quality about it."

The phenomenon of the timely but "timeless" *Room* did not escape the attention of international film awards committees. In England, *A Room* was voted Best Film of 1986 by both the Critics Circle Section of Great Britain and the British Academy of Film and Television Arts—with another award to Richard Robbins for Best Musical Score from the British Film Institute. In Italy, it was awarded the Donatello Prize for Best Foreign Language Picture, and Ivory was honored as Best Director. In America, *A Room* was nominated for eight Academy Awards, including Best Picture and Best Director; and it won three—for Best Art Direction, Best Costume Design, and Best Screenplay Adaptation.

MAURICE
(1987)

DURING THE PERIOD of *A Room*, Merchant Ivory contemplated making a documentary on the novelist Christopher Isherwood, then in his eighties, whom they had known in California and in the course of his work in the theater. As Ivory relates in his article "Isherwood" (*Sight and Sound,* Spring 1986), their idea was to move into his home with a small crew and follow him on his rounds for a month, letting him talk about past and present, and the many people he knew (Forster among them). Channel 4 in England agreed to underwrite part of the budget for the documentary, but the project stalled when the National Endowment for the Humanities turned it down, and it was then turned down again by the Corporation for Public Broadcasting, which funds Channel 13 television in New York, apparently because it would have "limited appeal to minorities"! The work

(opposite) The boat that Scudder missed.

(overleaf) Maurice and Clive riding at Pendersleigh. Actually, these are stunt riders Harvey Kip (left) and Adrian Ffooks (right). Film underwriters don't like it very much when principal players go galloping around on horseback, and often it is a question of whom to pacify: the insurance company or the furious, if foolhardy, actors, who are always ready to risk a broken neck.

As did Tom Cruise. He was somewhat surprised that at the end of Ruth's script he didn't get the girl. Cruise accepted our ending, however, because, he told us, it was what *we* wanted, and he was genuinely making the film, I think, because he liked us. JI

To some extent when *A Room With a View* came out in England, and to a lesser degree with *Maurice*, I was surprised, judging from reviews, at how little affection the English seem to have for Forster. It was as if we had taken something negligible and dated, something even a bit tiresome or dowdy, and made it amusing, stylish, high-spirited, or dramatic—had improved the source material almost out of all recognition. I was often asked by English interviewers, "What do you see in Forster?" JI

might yet have been made, except that Isherwood's health worsened. His death in December 1985 put an end to their chance to make what Ivory calls "the only film about Isherwood ever to be seriously attempted."

After *A Room*, Merchant Ivory next turned to the making of *Maurice*. But with the huge success of *A Room*, Merchant Ivory were in demand and it was a busy time; and two other projects, neither of which reached the screen, were initiated while *Maurice* was being made. One was the film *Woman Wanted*, a comedy set at Yale University that was to star Mia Farrow. It was to be made with MGM, produced by Richard Zanuck and David Brown (who had been the sympathetic executive producers of *The Guru*), and directed by Ivory. A script had been prepared, but Ivory and Joanna Glass, who had written the novel, wrote a new one that led to problems with the producers, who liked the original one better. Nor could Ivory and the producers agree on casting. "There was an uproar," Ivory told me, "over who would play the Yale professor. They wanted all sorts of inappropriate and unappealing people. I just could not agree to any of that, so they fired me."

During the same period Ivory became involved in a film project for United Artists, which was to be called *An Innocent Millionaire* and to star Tom Cruise. Cruise was to play an extremely idealistic young man who has a dream of finding a sunken treasure ship. But after he does find it, the treasure is gotten away from him by art dealers and other connivers; and the second half of the movie deals with the Cruise character's taking them to court and had, as Ivory says, "all kinds of wonderful courtroom scenes that I had always wanted to do." The studio was at first wildly enthusiastic about the script Jhabvala wrote until Stephen Vizinczey, the author of the novel on which the film was based, read and violently objected to it. "Then," Ivory remarked, "they got cold feet. They wanted the ending changed, and all sorts of things. We said, 'No, we won't do it.' So we dropped out."

These ventures, however, did not interrupt the making of *Maurice*, their adaptation of Forster's novel about a young man's awakening to his homosexuality in Edwardian England. It was Ivory who launched the project. While completing *A Room*, he reread all of Forster's books and eventually came to *Maurice*. "I thought," Ivory said, "that it was interesting material and would be enjoyable to make—and also something we *could* make in that it wouldn't require too much organization and wouldn't cost all that much." The situation it explores also seemed to him to be still timely: "People's turmoil, and having to decide for themselves how they want to live and what their true feelings are and whether they're going to live honestly with them or deny them. That's no different. Nothing's any easier, for young people. I felt it was quite relevant."

Jhabvala, who was involved at the time in writing her large novel *Three Continents*, was unavailable for the project. Ivory wrote the screenplay, instead, with Kit Hesketh-Harvey, who had previously

147

Mr. Ducie (Simon Callow) explains the mysteries of sex to the young Maurice (Orlando Wells).

written documentaries for the BBC. Especially important was that he had gone to the Tonbridge School and Cambridge, where Forster was educated, and knew the social background. Jhabvala was shown the script, however, and made suggestions for changes. On her advice that Clive Durham's conversion to heterosexuality while recovering from an illness in Greece was weakly motivated (a criticism voiced by many readers of the novel as well), an episode was created in which Clive's university friend Risley is arrested and imprisoned after a homosexual entrapment—enough to frighten Clive ultimately into marrying. But apart from this change, the screenplay follows the novel very closely.

The self-governing board of fellows of King's College at Cambridge, who administers the Forster estate, were at first reluctant to give permission to film *Maurice*. Their reasons had to do not with the novel's subject matter but the commonly held view of it as an inferior work. A film that called great attention to it could not, they felt, do

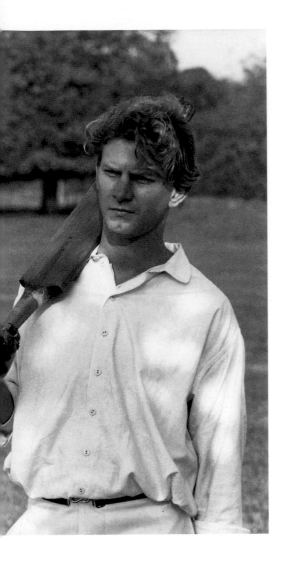

James Wilby, at the Pendersleigh cricket match.

Forster's reputation any good. Yet when Merchant conferred with them, he was very persuasive, and the company's adaptation of *A Room* had, after all, been impressive; and in the end they relented. In fact, they not only gave permission to Merchant Ivory to film *Maurice* but also allowed them to turn the college into a movie set. As it turned out, the fellows and students at King's College became extras, playing their Edwardian counterparts.

For Clive's estate, renamed Pendersleigh, Merchant Ivory were given the use for four weeks of Wilbury Park, one of the most beautiful Palladian houses in England. Its owner, Maria St. Just, an actress, friend of many people in the theater, and more recently a trustee of the estate of Tennessee Williams, had known Merchant and Ivory for some time. In 1979, they had been weekend guests at Wilbury Park, which made an impression on Ivory who, when *Maurice* was being prepared, felt that it would be right for Pendersleigh. Made on a budget of $2.6 million that included investment again by Cinecom and England's Channel 4, *Maurice* proved more complicated to make than Ivory had anticipated. Its fifty-four-day shooting schedule, which involved working six-day weeks, proved long and grueling.

Pierre Lhomme's photography takes full advantage of *Maurice*'s Cambridge and Pendersleigh settings, which appear with an opulent effect in such scenes as the candlelit dinner in Hall with Latin grace and the cricket match at Clive's country estate. Yet the visual texture of the movie has, as Ivory had asked of Lhomme, a "dark, cold, masculine look to it." With its dark tones and inclement weather, it gives the sense of a constrictive world that matches Maurice's own situation. Ivory pays close attention to Edwardian England's social and sexual codes that are revealed in telling and sometimes humorous moments—the don in the Greek class who tells his young men to omit "the reference to the unspeakable vice of the Greeks"; the hypnotist Lasker-Jones's attempt to convert Maurice to heterosexuality by conjuring an image of "Miss Edna May," a popular actress; and Dr. Barry's bearish refusal to listen ("Rubbish, rubbish") to Maurice's confession of his "criminal" feelings. The film works on two levels at once, as a realistic study of English manners that include ideas of class and as a psychological portrait of Maurice that at times has a romantic intensity.

Maurice has a faultless cast that includes Denholm Elliott as Dr. Barry, Simon Callow as the pedagogue Mr. Ducie, Billie Whitelaw as Maurice's mother, Ben Kingsley as Lasker-Jones, and Patrick Godfrey as the sneering servant Simcox. Hugh Grant gives a strong performance as the susceptible, class-conscious Clive Durham; but the great strokes of casting, I think, are James Wilby (chosen at the last moment when Julian Sands suddenly withdrew from the movie) as Maurice, and Rupert Graves as the cheeky under-gamekeeper Alec Scudder, a kind of genie from a bottle. Although conveying vulnerability, Wilby has a masculine presence that works against homosexual stereotyping; everything, in fact, about Maurice's relationship to Alec (including the nude, unapologetic love scenes) seems authentic and real.

151

(left) Maurice (James Wilby) and Alec Scudder (Rupert Graves).

(below) Risley (Mark Tandy) picks up a guardsman.

The hypnotist, Lasker-Jones (Ben Kingsley), puts Maurice into a trance.

Ivory allows the pair to have a basic dignity, to be an understandable part of human experience and desire; he accepts their homosexuality, which their society views with disapproval and condemnation, as being merely part of nature. One of the virtues of the film is its precision—its quiet, steady revelation of the oppressive formality in Edwardian society that keeps people apart, and the step-by-step inevitability of Maurice and Alec's desperation. Clive's marriage belongs to the Edwardian world he inhabits: it is made for appearances sake. Maurice and Alec, on the other hand, have a vitality that comes from trusting their emotions, acting against the grain of their surroundings. Some of the most memorable scenes are those moments when Maurice and Alec find release from their loneliness in their sexual "sharing," as Alec calls it. In many respects, *Maurice*'s themes are similar to those in *A Room*, although orchestrated differently. In *A Room*, which is about breaking free of conventional expectations for oneself, the nude bathing scene at the Sacred Lake contains Whitmanesque echoes of homoerotic liberation; and homosexuality, which was relevant to Forster in a very personal way, is a kind of subtext. In *Maurice* it becomes the full text, which Ivory has treated with intelligence and with a poignancy that is deeply felt.

At the 1987 Venice Film Festival, *Maurice* was honored with a number of awards. Hugh Grant and James Wilby shared the award for Best Actor; Ivory was corecipient, with Ermanno Olmi, of the Silver

Simcox (Patrick Godfrey), the insinuating butler of Pendersleigh.

Lion award for Best Director; and Richard Robbins won the award for Best Musical Score. The film drew strongly favorable notices when it opened in New York. Some critics objected to the fantasy ending in which Maurice and Alec go off into an unclear future in Forster's novel as well as Ivory's film. But the ending is effective in a number of ways. It is "magical," but magic has entered into the film previously when, for example, Alec enters Maurice's bedroom window, a scene that dramatizes the power of instinct to assert itself marvelously in a world governed by rationality and repression. In the ending, moreover, it is not only Maurice who is a focal figure, but also Clive, as he stares out the window of his bedroom at a vision of Maurice saying goodbye while his easily deceived wife waits for him to join her. The ending draws attention to the choices the characters make. It is the film's theme of self-realization, as against external pressures to conform, that

What could that future have been, actually?—within a year or two to end up in the trenches of the Great War. JI

Maurice is "platonically" embraced by Clive Durham (Hugh Grant).

(overleaf) Kit Harvey *(far left)*, author of the *Maurice* screenplay with Ivory, is put to work, along with the film's producer *(back to camera)* and his eight-year-old nephew, Rizvan Chawan. (1986)

gives *Maurice* its universality, beyond the issue of homosexual identity it speaks to so directly.

The theme of a growth to self-realization links *Maurice* with Merchant Ivory's adaptations of James and Forster that come just before it. Jhabvala's screen version of *The Bostonians* deals with self-deception and self-discovery for both Verena and Olive. Self-discovery comes to both of them and at the same time, as Verena leaves the Boston Music Hall for a domestic life with Basil Ransom and as Olive mounts the podium to become an active spokeswoman for women's rights. In *A Room*, Lucy Honeychurch, in conflict with herself, is forced to make choices that bring her to a realization of who she is. The film is a celebration of the value of the individual, and so in the painful choices forced on the protagonist is *Maurice*. The self-realization theme proves rewarding throughout this period in which Jhabvala and Ivory enter into a kinship with James and Forster. It seems very fitting that they should bring James and Forster to the screen, since they have much in common with them—in their interest in the subtlety and irony of human relationships, and in their humanistic perspectives on experience. In the trilogy of mid-1980s films, Jhabvala and Ivory reveal themselves in the finest sense as "literary" filmmakers, committed to novels that they have not only understood but also made anew.

155

CHAPTER VII

Entering the Nineties— the New York Art Scene and the Midwest Mainstream

THE DECEIVERS
(1988)

I N THE EARLY 1980s Merchant first set in motion a project of
which he had long dreamed, and that he was to do outside of his
usual collaboration with Jhabvala and Ivory, the making of *The
Deceivers*. *The Deceivers* is adapted from the John Masters novel, set in
India in 1825, which depicts the exploits of William Savage (based on
William Sleeman of the Indian Political Service), who disguises himself
as an Indian in order to expose and destroy a secret cult whose members, the infamous Thugees, ritually murdered and robbed travelers in
the name of the goddess Kali. Merchant had read the novel years
before, been struck by it, and later decided to film it. The movie was
slow in getting into production, however, and once into that stage presented such an array of problems as to stagger even Merchant. An
entire book, *Hullabaloo in Old Jeypore: The Making of "The Deceivers,"*
was needed for Merchant to set down all that occurred.

The $5.2 million final budget of *The Deceivers* was financed by
Orion Pictures, Cinecom (which had backed *A Room* and *Maurice*),
England's Channel 4 television, and other investors, including Michael
White, the successful British West End producer, who provided the
"seed money" for script development and other early expenses. But
years passed between initial conception and the completion of the
movie. A series of directors (Marek Kanievska, Stephen Frears) seemed

Hussein, a *thugee* (Saeed Jaffrey, *center*).

158

British troops to the rescue—or more correctly, the troops of the British East India Company.

Lieutenant William Savage (Pierce Brosnan).

committed to the project only to cancel out before Nicholas Meyer accepted the assignment, and a similar experience occurred with actors sought for the male lead (Christopher Reeve, Treat Williams) before Pierce Brosnan took the role. Finally production started and Merchant's problems really began—problems increased by the fact that he was forced to be away from India at different points: to be present at the American opening of *Maurice,* and to be a guest of honor at the twenty-fifth-anniversary tribute to Merchant Ivory by the American Film Institute in Washington, D.C.

A chief problem for Merchant in the making of *The Deceivers* was a man from Jaipur named Bonnie Singh. When Singh was not hired to work on the movie as a production location manager, he retaliated through a friend, who brought charges against the filmmaker in India's civil courts, claiming that the movie misrepresented Indian culture. After the charges (painful because Merchant Ivory's relations with the Indian government's Ministry of Information and Broadcasting had always been amicable) were dismissed as baseless, sets and camera equipment were mysteriously sabotaged, and then charges were brought against Merchant and his coproducer Tim Van Rellim in the criminal courts that echoed the earlier ones, while demonstrators whipped up hysteria by making claims that *The Deceivers* encouraged suttee, or widow burning. Policemen armed with machine guns came to raid Merchant's field office and arrest him (Merchant was crossing India by train at the time, oblivious of what was happening), and the incident was reported in the international press. Readers of *The New York Times* stared in disbelief at accounts of what was taking place. Eventually the unfounded charges were dropped, but these incidents, and much more than these, threatened to derail the film. Remarkably, Merchant managed to quell the troubles and to bring the picture in on schedule and on budget.

The Deceivers is an action-adventure film with an exotic setting and a solid, good-looking cast that includes Pierce Brosnan as Savage, and Keith and Helen Michell (the sister at whom Maurice lashes out in *Maurice*), an actual father and daughter, who play Colonel Wilson and his daughter Sarah. The Indian cast, which appears to include "thousands," features Merchant Ivory veterans Saeed Jaffrey as Hussein, who provides Savage with entrée to the Thugees, and Shashi Kapoor as the double-dealing Chandra Singh. Jenny Beavan and John Bright, who won an Oscar for their work in *A Room,* designed the colorful costumes, and Walter Lassally's photography gives *The Deceivers* a visual opulence that is impressive even by Merchant Ivory standards. The film begins at a British post but before long moves to the countryside where Savage, in Indian dress and his skin darkened with dyes, infiltrates the ranks of the Thugees or "deceivers," learning about blood lust at firsthand as he falls under the spell of Kali. Savage's journey into an Indian "Heart of Darkness" provides psychological tension that accompanies the suspense of events that swirl around him and end finally with a restoration of order.

William Savage turned *thugee*.

Much talent has been lavished on the film, but *The Deceivers* seems curiously old-fashioned, like a movie that might have been made by Alexander Korda; and it raises a number of never fully answered questions: Why, for instance, would Savage have undertaken such a dangerous exploit? Why, with such a distinctly English cut to his features, would he not have been discovered? What convinces us that he would speak the Thugees' dialect without slip? *The Deceivers* succeeds best on the level of its thriller surfaces, from chilling opening to stunning climax.

SLAVES OF NEW YORK
(1989)

WHILE MERCHANT WORKED ON *The Deceivers* outside of his usual Merchant Ivory collaboration, Jhabvala also undertook a project independently of the others, writing the screenplay of *Madame Sousatzka*, based on the novel by Bernice Rubens about an aging European woman in London who teaches the piano and her relationship with a boy who is her protégé. Jhabvala's involvement in the movie came about when her former agent in London, Robin Dalton, became a producer and came to her one day to ask if she would do the screenplay for John Schlesinger. Jhabvala was familiar with a number of Schlesinger's films but had just seen one about the British defector Guy Burgess, *An Englishman Abroad*, which particularly impressed her and made her decide to accept the assignment.

Madame Sousatzka, which starred Shirley MacLaine in the title role and opened in New York in October 1988, is fascinating when compared to Rubens's novel—for its transpositions, changes, and

(opposite) Eleanor (Bernadette Peters), slave, with Stash, slaveholder (Adam Coleman Howard), in his East Village loft.

One day we were shooting a dialogue scene in a taxi cab with Bernadette Peters and two other actors. For this we chose First Avenue, driving north from 10th Street to 14th Street, and then coming back down Second Avenue and starting over again. Just before we began shooting, there was a murder at the corner of First Avenue and 10th Street. A man had been shot while using a pay phone on the corner and now lay dead on the sidewalk. A little crowd had gathered. We kept going round and round on our route doing re-takes, and every time we passed, the crowd was smaller, until at the end only the corpse was there under a sheet, with a couple of detectives taking photographs and measuring. JI

reshapings. Jhabvala's screenplay is a model of craftsmanship that refocuses urbanely Rubens's story of the fragility of relationships. Interestingly, it carries over Jhabvala's themes for Merchant Ivory films of art and manipulation. Not only Madame Sousatzka but also the mother and the London music producer all vie with each other, out of needs or compulsions of their own, to possess in this case not a prized work of art but the artist figure himself, the talented young pianist.

Jhabvala had no hand in Merchant Ivory's next film, *Slaves of New York*, but she inspired it. She read Tama Janowitz's Eleanor and Stash stories in *The New Yorker* and recommended them to Ivory, who became interested in doing a film based on them. Andy Warhol owned the film rights to the stories, and Janowitz began a screenplay for him; but when Warhol died, Merchant bought the unfinished script, as well as the five stories in *The New Yorker* and the others included in Janowitz's best-selling collection. Janowitz admits that she had never really done a completed screenplay before: "There was something in the one I did for Warhol, but it needed structure and tension. I worked with Jim for about six months and learned everything from him."

Slaves of New York was coproduced by Merchant with Gary Hendler, ex-president of Tri-Star Pictures, which financed its $5.5 million cost. The association with Tri-Star proved a particularly happy one. Ivory refers to the Tri-Star executives as "gentlemen" who "never interfered," and did the movie "because we wanted to do it," not because they saw a fortune in it. The movie was shot entirely in New York, principally on the Lower East Side, in ten weeks. It proved demanding to make in many respects. Richard Robbins, for example, had to do a tremendous amount of research in order to select the music to be used. "I had to spend an incredible amount of time," he remarks, "trying to keep up with the latest in pop music. I spent thousands of hours in New York clubs listening to all kinds of music that I don't usually listen to in order to decide what would be right for the film." Because it deals with the art scene "downtown," its contemporary art work, scenic design, and costuming also involved elaborate preparation.

By the time of its release, partly because of its promotional tie-in with Bloomingdale's *Slaves of New York* boutique that featured fashions depicted in the film, the movie had become something of a media event. But the making of the picture was not always glamorous. Merchant recalls that shooting on 42nd Street, with its underclass of derelicts, "was like being swallowed into a hellhole," and that when they filmed on 14th Street, and traffic on the artery became snarled, people were abusive. While shooting in "Alphabet City," the lettered streets of the Lower East Side, the set became infested by drug dealers attempting to peddle their wares.

The New York opening of *Slaves* was a disaster: reviews were extremely harsh, the worst Merchant Ivory had known. It may be that *Slaves* was harmed by the Bloomingdale's tie-in ("unfortunate, unnecessary, unwanted," Ivory says), which influenced people to perceive the film more as an extension of the Bloomingdale's phenomenon than as

(*opposite above*) Johan Carlo and Michael Butler, performance artists.

(*opposite below*) The Supremes sing "Love Is Like an Itchin' in My Heart": more cross-dressing.

Ginger Booth (Mary Beth Hurt) with the irrepressible Marley Mantello (Nick Corri).

a work to be taken on its own terms. *Slaves* is flawed in certain respects (its characters do not have much dimension and its humor at times fails to come off by being too broad), but it is a good film that manages to be both light-hearted and philosophic about young artists in Manhattan. The world downtown that it creates is almost intolerable: rents have soared out of control and apartments are practically unobtainable. Moreover, the ambiance of the East Village itself, with its manic pace and media hype of the art being produced there, lends itself to dehumanization. The young artists of the area are all on the make; their use of others in order to advance themselves is practically a norm. Ivory stages a number of lively scenes at East Village night spots in which real human communication seems impossible. At one, with an effect of weird fantasy, a girl on stage in a bathtub filled with soap bubbles belts out a song while cleaning her inner ear with a carrot. At another the music is so loud and the strobe lights so blinding that Eleanor faints. These scenes evoke a self-enclosed subculture in which reality becomes shell-shocked.

In this milieu in which identity is difficult to establish, Eleanor has an uphill struggle. At the beginning she is dependent on her boyfriend Stash for a place to stay, and is hence his "slave"; she takes his assaults on her small ego. Ironically, she moves against the current of

her environment, seeking not celebrity but normality. "I'm a normal person," she cries, "I'm trying to achieve the middle class." What she wants most is a home. In earlier films of Ivory's, a home had figured prominently; in *The Europeans*, for example, the Wentworths' New England home had incorporated communal values. Even in *Jane Austen in Manhattan*, with its enclave of theatrical careerists, George Midash and Lilianna Zorska had, if not homes exactly, at least lofts that imply tradition and roots; his is furnished with antiques and harpsichords, and hers is full of theatrical memorabilia. But in *Slaves* homes have disappeared, or been replaced by transiently occupied apartments, if such can be found.

What one finds chiefly in the East Village art scene is disconnectedness of individuals from others, and at times from all reality. Disconnectedness is what one notices in Stash (Adam Coleman Howard); it is his self-absorption that makes him comic, prevents him from seeing how small he is. He paints pop art pictures of cartoon characters that he photographs from a TV screen and, in his failure to develop to adult awareness, seems like a cartoon character himself, rather like Ivory's film actors in *Bombay Talkie* or *The Wild Party*, whose personal lives mirror the roles they play on the screen.

As Stash's stature, never large at the beginning, diminishes through the course of the film, Eleanor's increases. Hers is a Cinderella story. A poor waif at the beginning, Eleanor (wonderfully played by Bernadette Peters) is touching and astray; but in a fairy-tale way she succeeds—finds a place of her own, some little success as a designer of outré hats, a scrap of identity, and a promising new boyfriend. The boyfriend Jan (Michael Schoeffling), who appears late in the film, is a sturdier figure than Stash: masculine in appearance, he also seems rather sensitive and, unlike the helpless Stash, can "do" things, "fix" things. At the end, Eleanor joins Jan on his motorcycle, and the tracking shot of them crossing one of Manhattan's bridges at dawn is a celebration of Eleanor's spirit of survival in the city. Yet the happy ending has a certain ambivalence since, only shortly before, Jan had once told Eleanor significantly that relationships almost never give what one expects from them.

Slaves draws on Janowitz's material but transforms it. Her stories belong essentially to black humor, giving a sense of bleakness and emptiness; at their best they have a sharp, unillusioned sense of place, but their horizons are narrow. The stories give no sense of a world in which traditional values may possibly exist in contrast to the ones in the East Village. The sensibility of the film, on the other hand, is Ivory's, and it gives a far greater sense of spaciousness. In Ivory's vision the idea of values, although never overtly stated, is implied; one is continually conscious of the downtown scene as a distortion of values that have existed in the past. Not only the East Village but also New York itself, captured graphically in the brilliant camera work of Tony Pierce-Roberts, looms as a setting in which values are in a state of fragmentation and near collapse.

(below) Abby (Tama Janowitz) and Eleanor, fresh from their hairdressers.

(opposite) Frenzied hat making at Daria's terrible birthday party.

(overleaf) Bernadette Peters *(left)*, and Madeleine Potter *(right)*. Wilfredo's big fashion show at the old Saint disco.

Ivory's vision is above all tolerant, observant, and suave. He juxtaposes panoramic views of the Manhattan skyline at dawn and dusk—provoking wonder in its richness and vastness—with close-up scenes of East Village confusion in which no one has any stable identity; he is a bemused and sometimes amazed observer of New York life in the 1980s. What is remarkable about *Slaves* is its double vision. Ivory reveals affection for his characters, is understanding of them, and even at times shows a certain insouciance in his treatment of them. Yet they, and the city they inhabit, are also subjected to the more distanced irony of his observation, with its very knowing awareness.

A film about the downtown art scene may seem like an odd or almost unaccountable departure for Ivory, but it belongs very much with his other work—partly in his interest, from as early as *Shakespeare Wallah*, in placeless or displaced people; people whose illusions or lack of anchoring in reality belong to a larger pattern of disruption in culture. If in *Quartet* Ivory's characters cannot become real, in *Slaves* they are deprived of a sense of identity by belonging to a world of "art" that has become a commodity; they are rootless, devalued people. In America, critics dismissed *Slaves* as trifling, but it was regarded differently overseas, receiving strong reviews in England and rave reviews in France. In his suite at the Ritz in Paris, Ivory was beseiged by reporters eager to interview the man who made the ironic, humorous, and statement-making *Slaves of New York*.

167

Mr. Perfect (Dinshaw Daji), cause of all the hullabaloo in *The Perfect Murder*.

THE PERFECT MURDER
(1990)

THE PERFECT MURDER, which premiered in New York at the Angelika Film Center in March 1990, was released under the auspices of Merchant Ivory Productions. But although Merchant is credited as its executive producer, having helped to arrange financing and distribution, he had little part in the actual shooting of the film. In the late 1980s, Merchant became interested in organizing an independent film unit in Bombay that would provide an opportunity for local film people to make modestly budgeted films for distribution in the West. *The Perfect Murder*, the first in a prospective series of films by this group, is a detective story with more than a small amount of humor, based on the British writer H. R. F. Keating's novel about Inspector Ghote (Go'-tay) who, with a Swedish criminologist studying Indian police methods, unravels a diamond-smuggling caper.

As with *The Deceivers*, the idea of making the film was Merchant's, who had read the novel "ages ago"; he brought the film into being for a scant $500,000. It was produced by Wahid Chowhan (Merchant's brother-in-law) and directed by Zafar Hai, a maker of documentaries who brings a documentary dimension, in both details and flavor, to the film. Photography was by Merchant Ivory cinematographer-of-choice Walter Lassally, and the musical score by the durable Richard

Lala Herra Lal (Amjad Khan), flanked by the two seemingly incompetent detectives who eventually charge him with diamond smuggling, if not with murder: *(left)* Axel Svenson (Stellen Skarsgard) *(right)* Inspector Ghote (Naseeruddin Shah).

Robbins. The movie stars Naseeruddin Shah as the mild-mannered Ghote; Stellen Skarsgard (Ingmar Bergman's Hamlet) as the Swedish Axel Svenson; Amjad Khan as Lala Heera Lal, an enormously fat, acquisitive builder and part-time dealer in contraband; and Madhur Jaffrey as Lal's intimidating wife. The story itself is slight but moves briskly, and it has some very amusing moments, as in the scene where Ghote introduces Svenson to Mrs. Ghote, "the perfect Hindu wife." She turns out to be a shrew full of stinging resentment at her husband's neglect of her to pursue his police work. Like Ghote himself, *The Perfect Murder* is a surprisingly gentle, unassuming film, the most eye-catching feature of which is the crowded, sometimes bizarre street life of Bombay. Madhur Jaffrey appears briefly, but her steely eyes—full of shrewdness, pride, and aggression—are wonderful to behold, enough to make even a strong man blanch.

MR. AND MRS. BRIDGE
(1990)

MR. AND MRS. BRIDGE grew out of a dinner in 1987, at which Ivory met Paul Newman and Joanne Woodward for the first time. Woodward brought up the subject of Evan Connell's *Mrs. Bridge*, which she said was one of the best novels she had ever read. She had, in fact, been trying, without much progress, to mount a television production of it. Ivory, who had read the novel years before and told Merchant at the time that it would make a good movie, expressed an interest in working on the project with the Newmans. Before proceeding further they needed a screenplay, to be written by Jhabvala, that everyone would approve. Jhabvala's screenplay, a conflation of Connell's classic novels *Mrs. Bridge* and its sequel, *Mr. Bridge*, pleased everyone. When Newman, after reading and liking the script, agreed to do the film, he attracted the money to make it. Cineplex Odeon, with whom Merchant Ivory worked for the first time, agreed to finance its $7.2 million cost—a bit high for a Merchant Ivory film, but as Merchant remarked: "If Paul and Joanne were to take their usual salaries, the budget would be $12 million."

Mr. and Mrs. Bridge held a special meaning for Ivory, who told an

(above) The Bridge house in the Mission Hills district of Kansas City—a descendant of the Wentworth house in *The Europeans*: clean, white, well-kept, buttoned-down, and Puritan—like Mr. Wentworth and Mr. Bridge.

(opposite) Caroline Bridge's high-school prom.

Walter and India Bridge in the bank vault (Joanne Woodward and Paul Newman).

interviewer that it was the only film he had made "about my own childhood and adolescence," and elaborated on what he meant in my conversation with him. It was not so much the country-club surroundings that were familiar to him, he said, as "the whole set-up, the town, the kind of mores, the way people thought, what went on at home, and the attitude of my father, so exactly like Mr. Bridge in some ways. It was in what people did in those days, their entertainment, their lives, everything about them. Klamath Falls, Oregon might have been a Wild West town, but in its way, a less pretentious way, a less citified way, it was an exact duplicate of life as described in the Bridge books. For instance, that luncheon table that Mr. Bridge went to in the Muehlbach Grill; my father used to go to a lunch table with all the lumbermen, a place called the Pelican Grill, and occasionally I would go there and also have lunch when I was a teenager. In no other film have I been drawing directly out of my early years."

174

A kiss refused: Douglas Bridge (Robert Sean Leonard, *center*), with his downcast mother and Eagle Scouts.

Jhabvala's screenplay, which went through two drafts and to which Evan Connell contributed suggestions for time and place verisimilitude, brings *Mrs. Bridge* and *Mr. Bridge* together seamlessly. Walter and India Bridge are, of course, the focal characters, appearing in almost every frame of the movie. But other characters from the novels also appear—the Bridge children: Ruth, the older, rebellious daughter played by Kyra Sedgwick; Carolyn (Margaret Welsh), a young look-alike of her mother in the film; and Douglas, played by Robert Sean Leonard, who had starred in another father-son relationship as the sensitive teenager who commits suicide in *Dead Poet's Society*. One meets Mrs. Bridge's friends Grace Barron (Blythe Danner) and Mabel Ong (Gale Garnett); her art teacher, the gentle, pathetic Mr. Gadbury (Austen Pendleton); the Bridges' maid, Harriet, given strong, attractive presence by Saundra McClain; and Mr. Bridge's nemesis, the psychiatrist Dr. Alex Sauer, played vivaciously by Simon Callow. These characters come together to tell the same tale, essentially, as the novels; and like the novels, the film has an episodic but very fluid movement, making it seem as if one were turning the pages of a family photograph album that tells the life story of the Bridges.

Paul Newman and Joanne Woodward blend into their characters so strongly that one can never again think of Mr. and Mrs. Bridge with-

(opposite above left) Ruth Bridge (Kyra Sedgwick) tells her father she wants to go to New York.

(opposite below) Walter and India Bridge approach the *Winged Victory.*

(above left) Cinematographer Tony Pierce-Roberts and Margaret Welsh, who plays Caroline Bridge.

(above right) Ivory and Paul Newman. (1989)

out thinking of Newman and Woodward. Woodward, still attractive in her late fifties, has been dressed in the clothes of the Thirties that give her the matronly appearance of a woman who may be well dressed but is unaware of chic. She is kind and well-intentioned, but too gentle to rebel against the rule of her husband or to find personal identity. As Walter Bridge, Newman has undergone a startling transformation; he has become rigid-jawed and stiff in his bearing, and acquired a lawyer's three-piece suit and wire-rimmed glasses. He is a handsome man still, but "square," lacking the flexibility in his work-driven life to express to his wife the emotions he feels for her. In *Mr. Bridge*, Connell writes that Walter Bridge married his wife shortly after her father died, "had taken her from the home where she had been sheltered as a child, and substituted himself for her father." The Bridge novels and the film show the effects of his sheltering of his wife, of keeping her a child. He is fearful of life, and she is unacquainted with it.

The movie is filled with wryly humorous moments. As a tornado bears down on the country club where the Bridges are having dinner, the other patrons hurry for shelter in the cellar, but Mr. Bridge, set in his ways to the point of absurdity, continues eating his meal. On their vacation to Europe, the Bridges visit the Louvre and seem comically out of place amid its paintings of vast size crowded with nudes. Yet the Bridges are also treated with respect and sympathy. In films as far back as *Venice: Theme and Variations*, Ivory had observed societies at a particular point in time, a time of change and transition; and *Mr. and Mrs. Bridge* focuses on that period in Kansas City between world wars when the restraints of an older world are being challenged by new mores. Walter Bridge is formed by the codes of the past and the economic pressures of the Depression, while a number of the other characters, and particularly their daughter Ruth, belong to the future, with its demand for openness and pleasure in life. Many of the finest moments in the movie are the shock points where Mr. and Mrs. Bridge are confronted by the sexual promiscuity of the young, by their rejection of accepted values, of them.

Mr. and Mrs. Bridge is the first of Merchant Ivory's films set in America to take place in its heartland, in the Midwest, and to be concerned with a well-to-do WASP family who represent it. A work of careful period reconstruction, it was beautifully photographed by Tony Pierce-Roberts, who filmed *A Room* and *Slaves;* but of all the settings none is more striking than the Bridge house, which is solid, gracious, and traditional. It is here that the film opens on a summer afternoon that is like an American idyll: in their backyard Mr. and Mrs. Bridge are enjoying themselves and their children are gathered around them. But the film moves from this summer idyl to winter at the end, where the home is the setting of Mrs. Bridge's loneliness.

The characters in *Slaves* might well have dreamed of a home like the Bridges' but it, too, is the setting of characters' disconnectedness from each other. Walter Bridge cannot bend, cannot display the love his wife so desperately needs. ("The saddest thing about Mrs. Bridge," Simon Callow told me, "is that she is a woman who could have been made happy very easily, but her husband withheld that little.") The children all grow away emotionally from Mrs. Bridge and have lives of their own apart from her. Her closest, most supportive friend, Grace Barron, feels emotionally stifled by her country-club life and commits suicide. In the end, the handsome but lonely house belongs to one of Ivory's major themes—an ideal in life that has been poignantly withheld.

In a very poised way, the movie balances humor with the sadness of Mrs. Bridge, who is so finely played by Woodward that one can smile at her helplessness and be touched by her at the same time. The film is also a gathering and restatement of many of Ivory's concerns— time and transience, society or a segment of it in its period manifestations, the conditions that make or thwart identity, the situation of the outsider (in a new variation of this theme the Bridges are "insiders" insofar as they belong to Kansas City's Establishment, yet "outsiders" to life). A surprising feature of the music is the minimalist sound, at least at times, of Richard Robbins's very striking and effective score. It makes one aware suddenly of a minimalist quality of many of Jhabvala and Ivory's films, with their attentive observation and consciousness of underlying tensions that create a kind of poetry in the real. The sensitive, mature *Mr. and Mrs. Bridge,* surely one of Merchant Ivory's best films, could almost be a summary of their art. *Mr. and Mrs. Bridge* opened in New York in late 1990 to a powerful showing at the box office and to rave reviews, often citing the film for its artistic finish. "With the quiet assurance of a perfect work of art," one critic wrote, "*Mr. and Mrs. Bridge* sweeps all other contenders off the screen to become the best movie of the year." The film also proved a triumph for Paul Newman and Joanne Woodward, whose performances were characterized by *The New York Times* as "the most adventurous and stringent of their careers."

CHAPTER VIII

New Directions

WHEN I INTERVIEWED Vanessa Redgrave in New York, I asked her what she considered especially distinctive about the film career of Merchant Ivory. It was, she thought, the consistently superior work they had done over the years. "It's difficult these days," she remarked, "when there are so few good scripts, so few films of substance, that are being made. With Merchant Ivory you have an opportunity to do a role that really interests you and that you care about deeply. You respect them for the spirit and the outlook that obviously guides their choice of films, and what they do, and who writes their films and who plays in them. They've got a record that literally cannot be matched. If anybody told me there was another company like them, I'd be amazed to hear it; there isn't any equivalent to them and what they do."

Especially during the last decade, Merchant Ivory has been identified in the public mind with award-winning literary adaptations that have been conspicuous for their faultless ensemble acting, imaginative casting, and choice of material. No one before them had ever attempted to bring *The Bostonians* to the screen, and until they proved it could be realized as a film, *Maurice* was considered a weak and unpromising property. Unlike the nice-to-look-at but stolidly literal adaptations frequently presented on "Masterpiece Theater," the adaptations of Merchant Ivory come to life freshly and with cinematic imagination. Annette Insdorf summed it up well when she remarked that Merchant Ivory "take the vast genre of literary adaptation and make it very personal and unique by choosing difficult material and treating it with as much intelligence as the original authors."

Merchant Ivory has been noted for its adaptations of Forster and James, but what is particularly interesting is that Jhabvala and Ivory have many affinities of sensibility with these writers. It is hard to think of another instance in which filmmakers have found their forebears, and found them with such certainty, in literature. Forster presents a special case, because his anatomy of Anglo-Indian relationships stands in the background of Merchant Ivory films set in India, but he is also relevant to Merchant Ivory films set elsewhere. Forster's great field is the novel of manners, with its concern with personal relationships in the context of the cultures to which the characters belong. He is rooted in the social situation, which he writes about with incisive wit and attention to complex shades of meaning. Merchant Ivory films share these concerns, and as in Forster they do not rush to make a point, being more interested in the texture of experience as it is revealed in gradual accretions. They mingle wittiness with psychological observation, and by the end their films compose a picture both of their characters and the societies to which they closely belong.

But their films also have affinities with James. Ivory has sometimes been called a "Jamesian director," and one writer has even gone so far as to imagine a composite individual named "Henry James Ivory." Comparison with James ought not to be carried too far. Neither Ivory nor anyone else has the shattering power of James's psychological imagination, his ability to create characters from the innermost depths of their consciousness. But Ivory does resemble James in his cosmopolitanism, his ability to enter into different cultures with detachment and discernment. Both are very civilized, are interested in manners (sometimes observed satirically), and have an elliptical approach to their characters in which what is left unsaid is often preferred to what is stated overtly. Some of James's concerns appear in Ivory's films, notably the international theme; but whereas James played off the Old World and the New (England and Europe versus America), Ivory plays off both Europe and America with the East.

I think at once of the collaboration between Satyajit Ray and his spiritual forebear Rabindranath Tagore, the Nobel Prize–winning author, to whose novels and short stories of nineteenth- and early-twentieth-century life in Bengal the director has returned again and again. JI

Hullabaloo Over Georgie and Bonnie's Pictures is a very Jamesian film in its exploration of ambiguous motivation, particularly among the Western connoisseurs of the fine arts who attempt to get possession of Indian art. But aesthetic consciousness, considered more generally, is a feature of James's fiction and Ivory's movies. The buildings in Ivory's films, their interiors, the clothes the characters wear, and the types and moods of the landscapes against which they appear all create a consciousness of the aesthetic that complements the refinement of Ivory's probing of his characters and their world.

The distinctiveness of Merchant Ivory films can also be illustrated in purely cinematic contexts. Ivory's familiarity with the work of other filmmakers, past and present, is extensive, but always among his favorites is Satyajit Ray. "Where Ray's concerned," Ivory remarks, "I feel an influence after all these years. I saw Ray's films and loved them even before I knew I'd do features, and then I began to do them, and by what now seems an extraordinary coincidence I found myself working in India with his cameraman Subrata Mitra, his assistant director Sailen Dutt, his soundman, his production manager, and others, too; and so naturally his influence came, in a sense, from the fact that he'd trained all these people who were working with me and, in a way, training me. That influence I still feel today because it's permeated everything I've ever done. What they and he taught me had more or less to do with things like timing and pacing, how to set up a scene, things like that. What I've unconsciously absorbed from him has remained with me no matter how much I've worked in the West and no matter how many films I've done that had nothing to do with Ray or India. I feel it and know I'm doing it somehow, though I may not recognize it at the time, or may recognize it perhaps later when I see their influence in the rushes or even in the finished edited scene."

Ivory's early films clearly show an indebtedness to Ray—*The Householder* in its quiet but luminous presentation of the lives of simple people to whom nothing very momentous happens; *Shakespeare Wallah* in its evocative sense of place with which the characters themselves seem to become fused. But Ray's influence persists beyond the early films in Ivory's meditative and distanced perspective on his characters, which can be noticed in films otherwise quite different in kind: it is in *Bombay Talkie, Savages, The Europeans, Quartet,* and *Mr. and Mrs. Bridge.* Ray once said that all his films were about time and change, and in Ivory's films time is also a preoccupation and is treated contemplatively. His films, like Ray's, are less interested in action of a flamboyant nature than in human behavior, in the sensitive revelation of character. Neither Ray nor Ivory assert themselves aggressively in their films, but instead reveal a kind of humility that permits their characters to come to life fully, with many emotional shadings of personality. Even the Alan sisters in *A Room with a View,* who do not have large roles, seem endowed with a certain largeness of life.

But if Ray provides a background for Ivory's work, Ivory uses what he learned from him to make pictures that Ray himself would not have made, films that have Ivory's stamp on them—personal,

Satyajit Ray on his set of *The Postman,* watching a rehearsal through the camera. (1960)

idiosyncratic, and unique. Over the years Merchant Ivory has made notable films of different kinds—movies about India, period films with diverse settings, social comedies, and shorts. With their Indian films, they led the way, exploring the Indian experience long before movies about India by other Western filmmakers came into vogue in the 1980s. These films reflect special credit on Merchant, who honored his homeland by helping to bring it into world cinema, as he had dreamed of doing while still a youth. As for social comedy, Merchant Ivory has created a special version of it, making it a vehicle for their intelligence and oblique wit.

Their films have sometimes been unpredictable: *Shakespeare Wallah* has the quality of the unexpected, and *Savages* could never have been foreseen; but *Jane Austen in Manhattan* is surprising, too. The settings of their movies shift back and forth between India, Paris, England, and America (New York and its outlying communities, Boston and New England, and the Midwest), as they orchestrate their themes in always changing social landscapes. Their movies have involved large social canvases as in *Heat and Dust*, and circumscribed subcultures as in *Slaves of New York* and *Courtesans of Bombay*. They have sometimes been interested in the lives of stage and screen actors, in the magic and the reality of the performing arts; and in cultures, like those in *The Europeans* and *A Room with a View*, in which art may have subversive connotations. But perhaps the chief thing to be said about their pictures is that they give pleasure of an original kind, setting a standard for others in the making of films that have a very personal quality rather than being predictable formula films produced in quantity by big studios. Their independent filmmaking over several decades has enlarged the dimensions of American filmmaking itself.

THE BALLAD OF THE SAD CAFÉ

BUT MERCHANT IVORY is not so much looking back as forward. A number of new films are planned for the near future and one, *The Ballad of the Sad Café*, from the novella by Carson McCullers, was shot on location in Texas. Although a Merchant Ivory film, *Ballad* is a project of Merchant's pursued (as he has done from time to time in the past) apart from his collaboration with Ivory and Jhabvala. The inspiration for it came to him as early as 1972 when Anthony Korner gave him the novella to read. Merchant was deeply impressed by it, but after inquiring into the rights, learned that they had been given by the McCullers estate to Edward Albee, who had adapted the work as a Broadway play in 1962; and that the play and the

The porch of Miss Amelia's general store, gathering place for those who buy her liquor.

rights to the novella had merged. Years passed while Albee waited for an interest in the property from a big Hollywood studio, but none materialized, and in 1988 Merchant acquired the option. By then Merchant had already discussed the project with Vanessa Redgrave, who admired the novella and was interested in taking on the challenging role of Miss Amelia. The financing of the $3.5 million project was underwritten in part by England's Channel 4 television, Curzon, and Joseph Saleh's Angelika Films.

I went out to Texas in July 1990 to see *Ballad* being made. The shooting location was a site in the country twenty-five miles west of Austin, on the ranch of the singer Willie Nelson. It had all the things Merchant needed, including a row of bleakly weathered, ramshackle buildings lining the main street of an apparently remote hamlet that Willie Nelson had used in a film of his own and that Merchant's crew had altered to give the appearance of a tiny town in the deep South. *Ballad*, which is Merchant Ivory's first film to be set in the American South, is quintessentially a tale of the South, belonging less to realism than to fable. Its story involves much grotesquerie: the tall, unfeminine Miss Amelia who rejects Marvin Macy on their wedding night; her later infatuation with a hunchbacked dwarf named Cousin Lymon;

Macy's return after years in prison to wreak vengeance on Amelia; and her retirement—like the ghost of the hamlet—into the shuttered seclusion of the decaying building housing the café where she had known a transient happiness. Beneath its surface peculiarity, however, *Ballad* deals with universal themes: the inequality of the lover and the loved, the chasm of incommunicability between people, the inescapable isolation in the human condition.

On the evening I arrived, I went to see the rushes of recent shooting at the location screening room, and there almost the first person I saw was Vanessa Redgrave. Since I had talked to her in the winter, she had undergone a startling transformation. Redgrave is a tall woman, but she seemed now to have grown taller still. Her hair, now bleached blonde, was cut short and brushed back from her forehead, making her look like a lank farmhand with haunting blue eyes. Although I was familiar with McCullers's story and had read the screenplay by Michael Hirst (who had earlier done the screenplay for *The Deceivers*), I was still not prepared for the overwhelming impression of androgyny that she gave and that, in the brilliant color of the rushes, was mesmerizing. On the set in the days that followed, I was impressed by scenes being shot with Keith Carradine as Marvin Macy and Rod Steiger as the Reverend Willin; but no scene struck me more than the one in which Redgrave wades waist-deep in a creek with the dwarf (Cork Hubbert) on her shoulders. It seemed to sum up the eerie poetry of the movie.

I discussed the making of the film with photographer Walter Lassally, doing his tenth movie for Merchant Ivory, and Simon Callow, the well-known stage actor and director and veteran performer in Merchant Ivory pictures, who was directing his first film. Callow is an exuberant man who talks enthusiastically about his conception of *Ballad*. The author of the 1988 book *Charles Laughton: A Difficult Actor*, Callow envisions the movie as a kind of homage to the only film Laughton directed, *The Night of the Hunter*, which is also set in a remote rural area and evokes characters and landscapes with a poetic, baroque stylization. "We've chosen a style," he said, "that deliberately heightens all the action, shot mainly in extreme close-up and long shot to achieve a kind of tableau effect that can be cryptic and mysterious. And, fortunately, I have an actress who is, I would say, the greatest living poetic actress—Vanessa."

Prior to its release in movie theaters in spring 1991, I attended a screening of *Ballad* and was able to see the totality of Callow's conception of the film. It is a daring one in which a suspension of disbelief is achieved in a hauntedness that pervades the Southern backwater locale and its inhabitants, who seem isolated from the rest of the world and are endowed with a kind of grotesqueness. Vanessa Redgrave as Miss Amelia dominates the film from beginning to end; in her strength and vulnerability, she has a heroic size possessed by none of the others. In her adoption of a quasi-masculinity, she has attempted to shield herself from life and love; but once in love—curiously with the

(above) Cousin Lyman (Cork Hubbard) arrives in town.

(opposite) Vanessa Redgrave, in a scene not included in the finished film.

(left) Miss Amelia and Marvin Macy (Keith Carradine) battle it out in the café.

freakish Lymon, who appears one day to claim a mysterious kinship with her—she comes to know the misery of the lover-misfit. Because Redgrave is compelling, the audience is made to share in the experience, as Merchant expressed it to me, of the "shattering" of her life.

One of the features of Callow's direction is that it makes one think at times of stage drama: it is very much the film of a man of the theater. The opening view of the revenant-like Redgrave in the upstairs window of the decayed building that once housed the café suggests a stage set; as do other settings in the film in which small, self-contained scenes occur—the tiny, weathered church in which Amelia and Marvin are married, and the café where Lymon and Amelia play host and hostess to the sharecroppers. In the manner in which these farm people surround, observe, and comment on Miss Amelia, one has the impression of a chorus, such as might be employed on stage. Moreover, the brutal, climactic fight between Amelia and Marvin in the café

(opposite) Keith Carradine as Marvin Macy and *(left)* with producer Ismail Merchant and Rod Steiger, who plays Reverend Willin.

could easily belong to the spotlighted stage center of a theater.

But at the same time Callow is attentive to the visual textures of the rural setting and employs many of the distinctive devices of cinema. The film is filled with striking images—like the face of Marvin Macy (when he is first introduced at the beginning of the flashback and is looking through a window at Miss Amelia) that is held for a long moment before fading from the screen, and the moment in which Amelia dances in the rain with the dwarf. Walter Lassally's cinematography, with its evocative bluish tints and burnished browns and golds, has exceptional richness; and Richard Robbins's musical score is extremely striking in its agitated rhythm and its large, symphonic sound that takes the story out of rural Georgia and gives it a broader framework that contains both fairy tale and universal experience.

Callow has directed the cast as an effective ensemble that includes

Three tough English stars in the Texas back country: cinematographer Walter Lassally, director Simon Callow, and Vanessa Redgrave.

the wonderfully gangling farm people who are dressed pathetically in coveralls and print dresses of the Depression period that look as if they had been ordered from a catalogue; Keith Carradine as Marvin Macy, whose love has hardened into hate; and Rod Steiger as Reverend Willin, who expatiates movingly—from the depths of terrible inner knowledge—on the difference between the lover and what he calls the "*beloved*." Probably the mythic power and somber beauty of McCullers's story can never be transferred fully to other, more objective media, but this *Ballad* has been far more imaginatively realized than Albee's stage version, and it represents a benchmark for Merchant. It is the strongest film, working apart from Ivory and Jhabvala, that he has done.

STREET MUSICIANS OF BOMBAY *and* IN CUSTODY

IN TWO OTHER FILMS in preparation, Merchant Ivory return to India. *Street Musicians of Bombay*, a documentary by Richard Robbins, has been partly shot and is expected to be completed and released in 1991. It came about when Robbins was staying in Bombay and woke one morning in his hotel room to hear singing in the street below. He went to the window and saw two street musicians, a leper couple, singing a duet of almost unearthly beauty. Fascinated by what he saw and heard, he conceived the idea of a film that would record street performers of various kinds, including jugglers, but chiefly musicians (vocal and instrumental) who live by meager handouts. In a larger sense, the film will document the street life of the city itself.

The second Indian film, to be set in Delhi and its outlying regions, is an adaptation of Anita Desai's novel *In Custody*, nominated for England's prestigious Booker Prize in 1984. It will be both produced and directed by Merchant. *In Custody* is a brilliantly crafted novel about a poor teacher named Deven who lives in a backward town called Mirapore and is a lover of Urdu poetry. He is commissioned one day by a publisher to do an interview for his magazine with the great poet Nur, who writes in Urdu. Deven's search for Nur and eventual encounter with him forms the basis of a sad, sometimes savage, comedy in which both men, committed to an elegant but dying language, become stranded in the past while contemporary India passes them by. The novel brings many ironic perspectives to its subject of idealism and reality, while giving a sharp sense of life as it is lived, at its lower edges, in Delhi and little Mirapore. Naseeruddin Shah, who played Inspector Ghote in *The Perfect Murder*, and Saeed Jaffrey will have roles in the film, which will be made for England's Channel 4 television and is scheduled to go into production in 1991.

(*overleaf*) Howards End, the country residence of the Wilcoxes, that serves as both the title of Forster's story and the focus of the film. This house, called Peppard Cottage in the real world, and minus the television antennae, is the film's most important set. It is located in Henley-on-Thames in Oxfordshire. Around 1900 it was owned by Lady Ottoline Morrell, who expanded its farmhouse core, put in gardens, and invited her famous artist friends and acquaintances here for weekends. These were often members of the Bloomsbury set, including Leonard and Virginia Woolf, Clive and Vanessa Bell, and Lytton Strachey. Augustus John used the converted stable for a studio, and there were also visits from Bertrand Russell, D. H. Lawrence, Henry James—and, E. M. Forster.

JEFFERSON IN PARIS

MERCHANT, IVORY, AND JHABVALA will also return to their accustomed collaboration in two feature films to be set in Europe. One of them, *Jefferson in Paris*, is about Jefferson's five years in Paris, from 1784 to 1789, as ambassador to France. It is the first Merchant Ivory film to be set in the eighteenth century and to deal with a great historical figure. The idea of the film came to Ivory from his reading, particularly of Oliver Bernier's *Pleasure and Privilege*, about eighteenth-century social life in the United States, France, and Naples. As France stands on the brink of revolution, Jefferson's personal life, his situation as a slaveholder, and the ambiguities of his personality are explored. A widower with rigid self-control, he is nevertheless drawn into a close relationship with Maria Cosway, the unhappy wife of a fashionable, philandering English miniature painter; and finally enters into a sexual liaison with Sally Hemings, a slave girl from his Virginia plantation. The subject of miscegenation will be a critical aspect of the film, but it is also intriguing to try to imagine from the screenplay what Ivory's visualization of prerevolutionary Paris and Versailles will be like.

HOWARDS END

MORE IMMEDIATELY IN VIEW is the filming of Jhabvala's adaptation of *Howards End*, the third in a series of films to be drawn by Merchant Ivory from the novels of Forster. Published to acclaim in 1910, *Howards End* is the most "modern" of Forster's novels. The Edwardian Age is presented dramatically at a point of crisis, and the novel has a scope that is large and comprehensive. In part a novel of ideas, it develops on different levels, so that the personal relationships of the characters are constantly implicated in the question of who shall inherit England. The novel deals literally with inheritance—of a house in the English countryside called Howards End owned by Henry Wilcox, whose affinities are with business and empire. With the exception of his first wife, Ruth, who is wedded to the house spiritually but dies early in the novel, the Wilcoxes are an unsympathetic clan, smug in their sense of property. Yet this family becomes closely involved with a very different one in the Schlegel sisters, Margaret and Helen, who have intellectual and humanitarian concerns. Indeed, Margaret becomes Henry Wilcox's second wife. In the complications that ensue, a class war is fought that reveals the characters and alters the destinies of all involved.

The class war depicted in *Howards End* takes place specifically within the middle class. The Wilcoxes are not aristocrats but people whose money comes from business interests and who belong solidly to the upper middle class; the Schlegel sisters, too, are middle class, but they are well enough off to be able to cultivate their interest in the arts and in social betterment; and Leonard Bast, the pathetic, down-at-heels clerk who enters into the lives of the Schlegels and, through them, of the Wilcoxes, occupies a place on the grim lower level of the middle class, clutching desperately at gentility as he is about to be swallowed into the abyss of poverty. In a virtually diagrammatic way, these different sets of characters all interact. Margaret moves upward in the class structure in marrying Henry Wilcox, while Helen moves downward in her involvement with Leonard Bast, whom she attempts to help. The intersecting lives of these characters bring discord and disruption, and lead finally to disaster, qualified by some hope of reconciliation at the end.

In both action and setting, *Howards End* is a novel of many patterns. The action, for example, moves back and forth between London and the countryside to give the sense of values in conflict. The city is used to evoke Forster's distrust of the emerging modern age, in which external forces work against social cohesiveness and lead to the depersonalization of individuals' lives. Houses figure prominently throughout the work. The Schlegel sisters have lived for many years in a comfortable but unassuming Victorian house in London where they have created a little pocket of order for themselves; but in the course of the work the house is torn down to make way for the new, anonymous apartment buildings that are being constructed in the area. The Wilcoxes own a number of houses but regard them largely as commodities; they view Howards End, for example, as merely one of the houses they own that can be added into the ledger of their worth. But to Ruth, Wilcox's first wife, it is endowed with meaning, representing both nature and tradition, the integrity of the inner or imaginative life. Significantly, Howards End is something more than a farm house but something less than an English country house; with a meadow that comes almost to its door, it mediates between society and a restoring rural tradition. All the patterns of the novel converge at Howards End, which comes to stand ultimately for England and its future.

Jhabvala's screenplay of *Howards End* is one of her finest, creating a sense of excitement as one reads on and the strands of Forster's narrative are brought together with a fluent realism. Without any sense of strain, she manages to capture the many disjunctions in the interweaving lives of the Wilcoxes, Schlegels, and Basts. Sometimes these disjunctions are quite humorous, as in the scene where the Schlegels' Aunt Juley Munt arrives at the railway station near Howards End in the mistaken belief that Helen Schlegel is to marry the Wilcoxes' son Paul (unaware that the sudden engagement had been broken that morning). She is given a lift to Howards End in the open motor car of the Wilcoxes' elder, arrogant son, Charles, who appears at the station through sheer coincidence and whom she thinks is Helen's fiancé. En route they talk at cross purposes, and when Aunt Juley's misconception is finally discovered, it merely leads to mutual anger and accusation; and the scene ends with Charles and Aunt Juley shouting at each other at the top of their lungs as the car disappears in a cloud of dust. The first approach of the Schlegels to the Wilcoxes ends in utter confusion.

Like Merchant Ivory's previous adaptations of Forster, *Howards End* involves the subtleties of personal relationships and a large Edwardian social canvas. But it is also a departure in some respects from *A Room with a View* and *Maurice,* both of which have overtly romantic themes. Its patterns are also more complex, and instead of having a protagonist who develops as a character by rejecting social conformity in order to achieve personal self-expression, it offers a central character in Margaret Schlegel, who grows in stature by assuming a role within the social order that brings the warring elements of society together with some kind of coherence. It is Margaret who speaks the novel's most famous phrase: "only connect," which is what, like Ruth Wilcox before her, she does, uniting the outward world of the Wilcoxes, with their superficiality but intractable power, and the Schlegels, with their sensitivity to values and allegiance to the imagination.

The filming of *Howards End* was prompted by Jhabvala; it is her favorite of Forster's novels, and she had always wanted Merchant Ivory to make the film—even before the company undertook *A Room with a View.* At this writing *Howards End* is in preproduction. Some of the roles have been cast—Vanessa Redgrave as Ruth Wilcox, the presiding conscience of Howards End; Anthony Hopkins as Henry Wilcox, her priggish but vulnerable husband; James Wilby as his unthinking, bullying son Charles; Emma Thompson as Margaret Schlegal; Helena Bonham Carter as Margaret's headstrong sister, Helen; and Sam West as the victimized Leonard Bast. If all goes as planned, it will be shot in England in the spring of 1991 and released in the spring of 1992.

All of these projects in various stages of development and production will bring Merchant Ivory into its fourth decade with a strong momentum. The forward direction of the company is suggested best perhaps in Merchant. He has a saying, "Don't look back." He contradicts himself in one respect, because he is fond of staging Merchant Ivory retrospectives; but what he means, of course, is that problems, setbacks, failures exist to be overcome and that the great thing is not to falter. He gives no sign today of faltering, has as many new projects in view as ever—more, he says, than can be contained "in one lifetime." What has impressed me most in my observation of him is that he is a man with a passion, an obsession with filmmaking that drives him relentlessly onward. When I think of Merchant, I think of the time I visited Ivory's house in the Hudson River Valley. Some guests had gathered on the front porch in the early evening, and when Ivory made a humorous remark, I noticed that, as Merchant laughed, his face brightened, giving him an expression of remarkable youthfulness. He is, I would say, a young man with a future.

We seem always to be having retrospectives—an embarrassing, immodest number of them. But I know they're necessary because they introduce our films to new audiences in places where they may never have been seen. I must say I groan whenever I hear that yet another retrospective is being planned, and that I'm expected to turn up there in festive dress. On these occasions I feel—and no doubt look—as battered as some of the earlier films themselves that we are presenting, films that can no longer be printed because the negatives are too fragile or have gotten lost and can only be shown in a discolored and much scarred, wornaway state, missing beats of music and important words. JI

Selected Bibliography

Adair, Gilbert. "Gilbert Adair from London." *Film Comment*, November/December 1980. Pp. 4, 6. (*Jane Austen in Manhattan*)

Arora, Nina. "The Dream Merchant from New York." *Film World*, February 1976. Pp. 42–43.

Bradbury, Nicola. "Filming James." *Essays in Criticism*, October 1979. Pp. 293–301.

Canby, Vincent. "A Partnership Waxes Strong." *New York Times*, September 25, 1983. Pp. 19, 26.

————. "Bostonians: A Proper Jamesian Adaptation." *The New York Times,* August 5, 1984. Pp. 15, 18.

Clarke, Gerald. "View from Prospero's Island." *Time*, January 12, 1987. P. 70.

Current Biography Yearbook 1977. New York: H. W. Wilson Company, 1977. Pp. 222–24. ("Ruth Prawer Jhabvala")

Current Biography Yearbook 1981. New York: H. W. Wilson Company, 1981. Pp. 228–31. ("James Ivory")

Daniels, Rebecca. "Not Slaves of New York." *Hudson Valley Magazine*, July 1989. Pp. 47–50, 85–86.

Eisenberg, D. "James Ivory and Ismail Merchant tell D. Eisenberg about their Wild Party with Raquel." *Interview*, January 1975. Pp. 10–11.

Giovannini, Joseph. "Merchant and Ivory's Country Retreat." *New York Times*, April 3, 1986. Pp. C 1, 8.

Gooneratne, Yasmine. *Silence, Exile and Cunning: The Fiction of Ruth Prawer Jhabvala.* Calcutta: Orient Longman, 1983.

Harmetz, Aljean. "Partnerships Make a Movie." *The New York Times*, February 18, 1990. Pp. C 13, 21. (*Mr. and Mrs. Bridge*)

Harrison, Barbara Grizutti. "The Subject is *Roseland*." *Village Voice*, September 26, 1977. Pp. 38–40.

————. "India, Inc." *Harper's*, March 1982. Pp. 65–70.

Hirsch, Allen. "*The Europeans:* Henry James, James Ivory, 'And that Nice Mr. Emerson.'" *Literature/Film Quarterly*, Volume 11, Number 2, 1983. Pp. 112–19.

Hunter, Allan. "Ivory Tower." *Films and Filming*, October 1987. Pp. 13–15.

Ivory, James. *Autobiography of a Princess—Also Being the Adventures of an American Film Director in the Land of the Maharajas.* New York: Harper & Row, 1975.

————. Introduction. *'Savages'*; a Film, by James Ivory, from a Screenplay by George Swift Trow and Michael O'Donoghue. *'Shakespeare Wallah'*; a Film, by James Ivory, from a Screenplay by R. Prawer Jhabvala and James Ivory. New York: Grove Press, 1973.

————. "Savages." *Sight and Sound,* Autumn 1971. Pp. 208–09.

————. "Hollywood versus Hollywood." *Index on Censorship,* Summer 1976. Pp. 10–12, 14–16. (*The Wild Party*)

————. "The Trouble with Olive." *Sight and Sound*, Spring 1985. Pp. 95–100. (*The Bostonians*)

————. "Isherwood." *Sight and Sound,* Spring 1986. Pp. 93–94.

————. , Michael O'Donoghue, and George Swift Trow. "Savages: A Motion Picture Outline." *Paris Review.* Summer 1972. Pp. 173–82.

Jack, Ian. "The Foreign Travails of Mrs. Jhabvala." *The New York Times Magazine,* July 13, 1960. Pp. 32–36.

Jhabvala, Ruth Prawer. *Amrita* (novel). New York: Norton, 1956. (Published in England as *To Whom She Will.*)

————. *The Nature of Passion* (novel). New York: Norton, 1957.

————. *Esmond in India* (novel). New York: Norton, 1958.

————. *The Householder* (novel). New York: Norton, 1960.

————. *Get Ready for Battle* (novel). New York: Norton, 1963.

————. *Like Birds, like Fishes, and Other Stories* (short stories). New York: Norton, 1964.

————. *A Backward Place* (novel). New York: Norton, 1965.

————. *A Stronger Climate: Nine Stories* (short stories). New York: Norton, 1968.

————. *An Experience of India* (short stories). New York: Norton, 1972.

————. *Travelers* (novel). New York: Harper & Row, 1973. (Published in England as *A New Dominion.*)

————. *How I Became a Holy Mother, and Other Stories* (short stories). New York: Harper & Row, 1976.

————. *Heat and Dust* (novel). New York: Harper & Row, 1977.

————. *In Search of Love and Beauty* (novel). New York: Morrow, 1983.

————. *Out of India* (short stories). New York: Morrow, 1986.

————. *Three Continents* (novel). New York: Morrow, 1988.

————. *The Householder* (screenplay). Delhi: Ramlochan Books, 1965.

————. *Shakespeare Wallah* (screenplay), in *'Savages'*; a Film, by James Ivory, from a Screenplay by George Swift Trow and Michael O'Donoghue. *'Shakespeare Wallah'*; a Film, by

James Ivory, from a Screenplay by R. Prawer Jhabvala and James Ivory. New York: Grove Press, 1973.

————. *Autobiography of a Princess* (screenplay), in James Ivory, compiler, *Autobiography of a Princess—Also Being the Adventures of an American Film Director in the Land of the Maharajas.* New York: Harper & Row, 1975.

————. "Disinheritance" (text of Jhabvala's Neil Gunn lecture). *Blackwood's Magazine,* July 1979. Pp. 4–14.

————. "An Experience of India." *Encounter,* Volume 31, Number 2, 1971. Pp. 3–15. (Also appears as Introduction to *An Experience of India.*)

Kendal, Geoffrey. *The Shakespeare Wallah: the Autobiography of Geoffrey Kendal.* London: Sidgwick & Jackson, 1986.

Lassally, Walter. *Itinerant Cameraman.* London: John Murray, 1987. Pp. 172–206. (Chapter 8, "Merchant Ivory")

Maychick, Diana. "Merchant of Magic." *New York Post*, January 18, 1989. Pp. 23, 32.

McFarlane, Brian. "Some of James Ivory's Later Films." *Cinema Papers,* June 1982. Pp. 214–19, 287, 289.

Merchant, Ismail. *Ismail Merchant's Indian Cuisine.* New York: St. Martin's Press, 1986.

————. *Hullabaloo in Old Jeypore: The Making of 'The Deceivers.'* New York: Doubleday, 1988.

Morais, Richard D. "Producer with a View." *Forbes*, March 23, 1987. Pp. 68–70.

Pym, John. "Heat and Industry." *Sight and Sound*, Summer 1982. Pp. 199–201. (*Heat and Dust*)

————. *The Wandering Company: Twenty-One Years of Merchant Ivory.* New York: British Film Institute/The Museum of Modern Art, 1983.

Shapiro, Harriet. "The Teeming Imagination of Novelist Ruth Prawer Jhabvala Is Her Window on a World She Avoids." *People* magazine, September 28, 1987. Pp. 48–50, 53.

Sucher, Laurie. *The Fiction of Ruth Prawer Jhabvala: The Politics of Passion.* New York: St. Martin's Press, 1990.

Tessier, M. "James Ivory: un cinéaste entre deux mondes." *Ecran*, April 1973. Pp. 1–9.

Trojan, Judith. "The Merchant Ivory Synthesizers." *Take One*, May 1975. Pp. 14–17.

Wakeman, John, ed. *World Film Directors: Volume Two: 1945–1985.* New York: H. W. Wilson Company, 1988. Pp. 458–65. ("James Ivory")

Watts, Janet. "Three's Company."

Observer Magazine, June 17, 1979. Pp. 61–65.

———. "The Million Dollar Merchant." *International Herald Tribune*. July 19/20, 1986. Weekend Section, p. 1.

Weinraub, Bernard. "The Artistry of Ruth Prawer Jhabvala." *The New York Times Magazine*. September 11, 1983. Pp. 64–65.

Villien, Bruno. "*Quartet.*" *Avant-Scène*, October 1981. Pp. 3–20, 32–50. (Special issue: discussion, film script, excerpts from French reviews)

Filmography

VENICE: THEME AND VARIATIONS

Director: James Ivory. *Producer:* James Ivory. *Script:* James Ivory. *Photography:* James Ivory. *Additional photography:* Stelios Roccos. *Editor:* Stelios Roccos. *Narration:* Alexander Scourby. *Production collaboration:* Museum of Fine Arts, Boston; California Palace of the Legion of Honor, San Francisco; Galleria dell' Accademia, Venice; Los Angeles County Museum; Metropolitan Museum of Art; National Gallery of Art, Washington, D.C.; Procuratoria di San Marco, Venice; San Diego Art Museum; Byzantine Society of Records and Byzantine Chorale (under the direction of Frank Desby); Sileno Corsini; Curtis Publishing Company, Philadelphia; Harper & Brothers, New York; Lester Novros; Anita Peabody; Saul Steinberg; Mrs. Diego Suarez; University of Southern California, Department of Cinema.
Running time: 28 minutes. *Filmed:* Venice, and museums and private collections as noted. 1952–1956. Color.
First distributed by Film Images, New York. March 1957.

THE SWORD AND THE FLUTE

Director: James Ivory. *Producer:* James Ivory. *Script:* James Ivory. *Photography:* Mindaugis Bagdon. *Editor:* James Ivory. *Music:* Ustad Ali Akbar Khan, Ravi Shankar, T. Visvanathan, Chatur Lal, D. R. Parvatikar. *Sound recording:* Rolf Epstein. *Special production assistant:* Raymond E. Lewis. *Narration:* Saeed Jaffrey. *Production collaboration:* Museum of Fine Arts, Boston; Freer Gallery, Washington, D.C.; Metropolitan Museum of Art; Hyman Bloom; Richard Bock; Charles Campbell; Mr. and Mrs. William P. Cleary; Dr. and Mrs. D. I. Elterman; Ratna Fabri; Roger Malek; Robert Marquis; Anita M. Peabody; James Rubin.
Running time: 24 minutes. *Filmed:* museums and private collections as noted. 1957–1959. Color.

First distributed by Film Images, New York. April 1959.

THE CREATION OF WOMAN

Trident Films. *Director:* Charles Schwep. *Producer:* Ismail Merchant. *Script:* Charles Schwep. *Photography:* Wheaton Galentine. *Art director:* Jim McIntyre. *Choreography:* Bhaskar Roy Chaudhuri. *Narration:* Saeed Jaffrey. *Cast:* Bhaskar Roy Chaudhuri, Dinu, Anjali Devi.
Running time: 14 minutes. *Filmed:* New York City, 1960. Color.
Released by Janus Films. Fine Arts Theater, Los Angeles. December 1960.

THE HOUSEHOLDER

Merchant Ivory Productions. *Director:* James Ivory. *Producer:* Ismail Merchant. *Screenplay:* Ruth Prawer Jhabvala, from her novel. *Photography:* Subrata Mitra. *Music:* Ustad Ali Akbar Khan. *Editor:* Pran Mehra. *Production coordinator:* Sailen Dutt. *Production controller:* Riaz Hafizka. *Production managers:* Bhanu Ghosh, N. Kabir. *Assistant director:* Prayag Raaj. *Translation Hindi version:* R. G. Anand. *Assistant camera operators:* Fatik Mazumdar, Joy Mitra, Shankar Chatterji. *Assistant editor:* Raja Ram Khotle. *Music assistant:* Jai Dev. *Incidental music:* Jyotirindra Moitra, Vanraj Bhatia. *Costumes:* Bettina Gill. *Makeup:* Nath Grover. *Sound recording:* Sujeet Sarkar, N. Mehta. *Sound re-recording:* Kaushik.
Cast: Shashi Kapoor (Prem Sagar), Leela Naidu (Indu), Durga Khote (Prem's mother), Achla Sachdev (Mrs. Saigal, the Landlady), Harendranath Chattopadaya (Mr. Chadda), Pahari Sanyal (the Swami), Romesh Thapar (Mr. Khanna), Walter King (the Professor), Patsy Dance (Kitty), Indu Lele (Mrs. Khanna), Prayag Raaj (Raj), Pincho Kapoor (Mr. Saigal), Praveen Paul and Usha Amin (Ladies gossiping), Shama Beg (Raj's wife), Pro-Sen (Sohanlal), Jabeen Jalil (Bobo), Ernest Castaldo (Ernest).
Running time: 101 minutes. Black-and-white. *Filmed on location:* Delhi, Mehrauli, Ghaziabad. March–August 1962.
Released by Columbia Pictures. Guild Theater, New York. October 1963.

THE DELHI WAY

The Asia Society, New York. *Director:* James Ivory. *Producer:* James Ivory. *Assistant director:* Toon Ghose. *Script:* James Ivory. *Photography:* James Ivory. *Music:* Ustad Vilayat Khan and Pandit Shantaprasad. *Editor:* James Ivory. *Production assistants:* Maniza Boga, Daphne Ghose, Ratna Fabri, Charles O. Hyman, Saeed Jaffrey, Madhur Jaffrey, Michael Jorrin, Jennifer Kapoor, Awtar Kaul, Ismail Merchant, Subrata Mitra, Robert Skelton. *Narration:* Leo Genn. *Produc-

tion collaboration:* Royal Library, Windsor Castle; National Film Archive, British Film Institute; Department of Archaeology, Government of India; Indian Office Library; British Museum; Stuart C. Welch, Jr.
Running time: 50 minutes. *Filmed:* Delhi. January 1960–January 1963. Color.
First Distributed by Film Images, New York. June 1964.

SHAKESPEARE WALLAH

Merchant Ivory Productions. *Director:* James Ivory. *Producer:* Ismail Merchant. *Screenplay:* Ruth Prawer Jhabvala and James Ivory. *Photography:* Subrata Mitra. *Music:* Satyajit Ray. *Editor:* Amit Bose. *Assistant to producer:* Mohammed Shafi. *Production manager:* N. Kabir. *Assistant directors:* Prayag Raaj, R. Shukla. *Assistant camera operators:* Fatik Mazumdar, N. Sarkar. *Assistant editor:* K. L. Naik. *Choreography:* Sudarshan. *Costumes:* Jennifer Kendal. *Makeup:* Nath Grover. *Sound editor:* Prabhakar Supare. *Sound recording:* Dev Roy. *Sound re-recording:* Mangesh Desai. *Production assistants:* Abbas Khan, Ali Raza.
Cast: Shashi Kapoor (Sanju), Geoffrey Kendal (Tony Buckingham), Laura Liddel (Carla), Felicity Kendal (Lizzie), Madhur Jaffrey (Manjula), Jim Tytler (Bobby), Prayag Raaj (Sharmaji), Pincho Kapoor (Guptaji), Partap Sharma (Aslam, the juvenile lead), Praveen Paul (Didiji, Manjula's companion), Utpal Dutt (the Maharaja), Hamid Sayani (Deputy Headmaster), Jennifer Kendal (Mrs. Bowen), Marcus Murch (Dandy in *The Critic*), Ismail Merchant (Theater Owner), Sudarshan (Manjula's Dance Director).
Running time: 120 minutes. Black-and-white. *Filmed on location:* Kasauli, Simla, Alwar, Lucknow, Bombay. September 1964–January 1965.
World Premiere: Berlin Film Festival, June 1965. *Winner of* Silver Bear for Best Actress (Madhur Jaffrey).

THE GURU

Arcadia Films/Merchant Ivory Productions, for 20th Century Fox. *Director:* James Ivory. *Producer:* Ismail Merchant. *Screenplay:* Ruth Prawer Jhabvala and James Ivory. *Photography:* Subrata Mitra. *Music:* Ustad Vilayat Khan. *Editor:* Prabhakar Supare. *Art directors:* Bansi Chandragupta and Didi Contractor. *Associate producers:* Muriel Neff, Peter Reilly. *Production controller:* Giancarlo Pettini. *Production manager:* Riaz Hafizka. *Location manager:* Rashid Abbasi. *Assistant directors:* Prayag Raaj, Mohammed Shafi, Wasi Khan, Shama Habibullah. *Assistant camera operators:* Fatik Mazumdar, Prajanan Mitra. *Assistant editors:* K. L. Naik, Humphrey

Dixon, Shri Ghate, Chris Crane. *Unit photographer:* Douglas Webb. *Songs:* "Tom's Boat Song" by Ustad Imrat Hussein Khan and Ruth Prawer Jhabvala; "Where Did You Come From?" by Mark London and Don Black. *Costumes:* Narender Kocher; (Michael York) Gordon Deighton; (Rita Tushingham) Joanna Tyson; (Leela Naidu) Malabar, Bombay. *Makeup:* Tony Delaney, Nath Grover. *Sound editors:* Don Ranasinghe, Brian Blamey. *Sound recording:* Dev Roy, Prabhat Das.
Cast: Utpal Dutt (Ustad Zafar Khan), Michael York (Tom Pickle), Rita Tushingham (Jenny), Madhur Jaffrey (Begum Sahiba), Aparna Sen (Ghazala), Leela Naidu (Girl at the Party), Zohra Segal (Mustani), Saeed Jaffrey (Murad), Usha Katrak (Lady Reporter), Fred Ohringer (Howard), Nargis Cowasji (Society Hostess), Marcus Murch (Snide Guest), Barry Foster (Chris Todd), Dorothy Strelsin (Tourist), Ismail Merchant (Compere), Rafi Ameer (Arnold D'Mellow), Soni Aurora (Teen Queen), Nana Palsikar (the Guru's Guru), Nadira (Courtesan), Pincho Kapoor (Murderer), Shri Agarwal (Doctor), Prayag Raaj (Classical Singer).
Running time: 112 minutes. DeLuxe Color. *Filmed on location:* Bombay, Bikaner, Benares. December 1967–April 1968.
Released by 20th Century Fox. 72nd Street Playhouse, New York, April 1969.

BOMBAY TALKIE

Merchant Ivory Productions. *Director:* James Ivory. *Producer:* Ismail Merchant. *Screenplay:* Ruth Prawer Jhabvala and James Ivory. *Photography:* Subrata Mitra. *Music:* Shankar Jaikishan. *Editor:* David Gladwell. *Art director:* A. Ranga Raj. *Production controller:* Mohamed Shafi. *Production manager:* Narendra Kumar. *Assistant production manager:* Abbas Shaiku. *Assistants to producer:* Mohan Nadkarni, Asha Seth. *Assistant directors:* Tom Reeves, Awtar Kaul, Shama Habibullah. *Continuity:* Janine Bharucha. *Assistant camera operator:* Adeeb Tandon. *Production artist/ titles:* Tilak Raj. *Songs:* Hasrat Jaipuri. *Playback singers:* Asha Bhonsle, Kishore Kumar, Mohammed Rafi. *Choreography:* Sudarshan Dhir. *Costumes:* Shaikh Hasan. *Makeup:* Nath Grover. *Sound editor:* Prabhakar Supare. *Assistant sound editors:* K. N. Chaven and Manohar Redij. *Sound recording:* Narendra Singh. *Sound re-recording:* Manghesh Desai, A. K. Parmar. *Adviser:* J. F. Van Der Auwera. *Film Extract:* "Naina."
Cast: Shashi Kapoor (Vikram), Jennifer Kendal (Lucia Lane), Zia Mohyeddin (Hari), Aparna Sen (Mala), Utpal Dutt (Bose), Nadira (Anjana Devi, Vikram's confidante), Pincho Kapoor (Swamiji), Helen (Heroine in Gold), Usha Iyer (Cabaret Singer), Sulochana (Gopal Ma),

Prayag Raaj (Director), Jalal Agha, Anwar Ali and Mohan Nadkarni (Anjana's young men), Sukhdev and Harbans Darshan (Men at Bar), Mirza Musharaff (Fan), Soni Aurora (Heroine in Red), Peter Howard, Angelika Saleh, Nicholas Lear, Tom Reeves, and David Gladwell (Ashram Inmates), Iftekhar (Vizarat Khan), Kamala Mehra (Operator), Datta Ram (Playback Singer), Mohan Dingra (Jeweler), Saudagar Singh and Vasant Singh (Wrestlers), Avadh N. Singh (Referee), Shama Hussein and Indu Lele (Two Ladies), Louis de Souza (Louis, the servant), Ismail Merchant (Fate Machine Producer).
Running time: 105 minutes. Eastman Color. *Filmed on location:* Bombay, Elephanta. January–March 1970 and July 1970.
Released by Angelika Films. Little Carnegie, New York, October 1970.

ADVENTURES OF A BROWN MAN IN SEARCH OF CIVILIZATION

Merchant Ivory Productions. *Director:* James Ivory. *Producer:* Ismail Merchant. *Script:* James Ivory. *Photography:* Walter Lassally. *Editor:* Kent McKinney. *Production associate:* Anthony Korner. *Sound:* Peter Sutton, Peter Rann. *Production assistant:* Richard Macrory. *Narrator:* Barry Foster. With Nirad C. Chaudhuri.
Running time: 54 minutes. Color. Filmed on location: Oxford, London, Chiswick. October 1970.
First Broadcast: BBC 2 (England), April 1, 1972.

SAVAGES

Angelika Films in association with Merchant Ivory Productions. *Director:* James Ivory. *Producer:* Ismail Merchant. *Screenplay:* George Swift Trow and Michael O'Donoghue, based on an idea by James Ivory. *Photography:* Walter Lassally. *Music:* Joe Raposo. *Editor:* Kent McKinney. *Art directors:* James D. Rule and Jack Wright. *Costumes:* Susan Schlossman and Joan Hanfling. *Executive producer:* Joseph J. M. Saleh. *Associate producer:* Anthony Korner. *Production manager:* Jean-Luc Botbol. *Assistant directors:* Jeffrey Jacobs, Stephen Varble, Nathaniel Tripp, Serge Nivelle. *Continuity:* Janet Kern. *Assistant camera operators:* Jeffrey Bolger, Robert Kenner. *Assistant editor:* Mary Brown. *Assistant art director:* Susan Middeleer. *Illustration and titles:* Charles E. White III. *Lettering and title design:* Michael Doret. *Assistant lettering and title design:* Edward Robbins. *Song:* "Savages" by Michael O'Donoghue, George Swift Trow, sung by Bobby Short. *Choreography* ("Steppin' on the Spaniel"): Patricia Birch. *Makeup:* Gloria Natale. *Hairstyles:* Martin Downey. *Sound:* Gary Alper. *Sound assistant:* John Flynn. *Sound*

re-recording: Jack Cooley. *Production assistants:* Frank Di Bari, Howard Goodman, Roger Moorey, Mohan Nadkarni, S. Ruth Gringras, Rick Raphael, Dustin Smith, Robin Schwartz, Emanuel Olivencia, Alice Marsh. *Narrators:* Lilly Lessing, Claus Jurgen.
Cast: Louis Stadlen (Julian Branch, a songwriter), Anne Francine (Carlotta, a hostess), Thayer David (Otto Nürder, a capitalist), Susie Blakely (Cecily, a debutante), Russ Thacker (Andrew, an eligible young man), Salome Jens (Mrs. Emily Penning, a woman in disgrace), Margaret Brewster (Lady Cora), Neil Fitzgerald (Sir Harry), Eva Saleh (Zia, the child), Ultra Violet (Iliona, a decadent), Asha Puthli (Asha, the forest girl), Martin Kove (Archie, a bully), Kathleen Widdoes (Leslie), Christopher Pennock (Hester), Sam Waterston (James, the limping man), Paulita Sedgwick (Penelope, a high-strung girl).
Running time: 106 minutes. Color. *Filmed on location:* Scarborough, New York. May–June 1971, April 1972. *World Premiere:* Cannes Film Festival. May 1972. (Director's Fortnight)

HELEN, QUEEN OF THE NAUTCH GIRLS

Merchant Ivory Productions. *Director:* Anthony Korner. *Producer:* Ismail Merchant. *Script:* James Ivory. *Additional photography:* R. M. Rao, Anwar Siraj. *Editor:* Andrew Page. *Narration:* Anthony Korner. *Film extracts:* Prince Jahan Pirar Milay, Gumnam, Nadan, Sachhai, Intequam, Caravan, Howrah Bridge, Sinbad Alladin Alibaba, Bombay Talkie. With Helen.
Running time: 31 minutes. Parts in color. *Filmed on location:* Bombay. January 1971.
First shown: Museum of Modern Art, New York City. March 1973. (New Directors Series)

MAHATMA AND THE MAD BOY

Merchant Ivory Productions. *Director:* Ismail Merchant. *Producer:* Ismail Merchant. *Script:* Tanveer Farooqi. *Photography:* Subrata Mitra. *Music:* Suman Raj. *Editor:* Andrew Page. *Art director:* Bansi Chandragupta. *Assistant camera operator:* Abid Tandon. *Sarangi player:* Ram Narayan. *Makeup:* Ragunath Parwar. *Sound:* Madan Prakash. *Sound re-recording:* Peter Rann.
Cast: Sajid Khan (the Mad Boy), Sulochanna (the Woman Feeding a Dog), Shastri (the Ghandi-ite Speaker), the people of Juhu Beach.
Running time: 27 minutes. Color. *Filmed on location:* Juhu Beach (Bombay). July to August 1972.
Released by Contemporary Films. Gate Cinema, London. March 1974.

AUTOBIOGRAPHY OF A PRINCESS

Merchant Ivory Productions. *Director:*

James Ivory. *Producer:* Ismail Merchant. *Screenplay:* Ruth Prawer Jhabvala. *Photography:* Walter Lassally. *Music:* Vic Flick. *Editor:* Humphrey Dixon. *Art director:* Jacquemine Charrot-Lodwige. *Assistant director:* Nick Young. *Continuity:* Christine Fox. *Assistant art director:* Richard Macrory. *Sound recording:* Bob Bentley.
Cast: James Mason (Cyril Sahib), Madhur Jaffrey (the Princess), Keith Varnier (Delivery Man) Diane Fletcher (Seductress), Timothy Bateson (Blackmailer), Johnny Stuart (Photographer), Nazrul Rahman (Papa).
Running time: 59 minutes. Color. *Filmed on location:* Kensington, London. March 1974.
World Premiere: New York Film Festival, October 1975. *Broadcast by* Public Television (Channel 13, New York) following the New York Festival.

THE WILD PARTY

Lansbury-Beruh/Merchant Ivory Productions. (A Samuel Z. Arkoff presentation, released through American International Pictures.) *Director:* James Ivory. *Producer:* Ismail Merchant. *Screenplay:* Walter Marks, based on the narrative poem by Joseph Moncure March. *Photography:* Walter Lassally. *Music/Music director:* Larry Rosenthal. *Editor:* Kent McKinney. *Art director:* David Nichols. *Executive producers:* Edgar Lansbury, Joseph Beruh. *Associate producer:* George Manasse. *Assistant director:* Edward Folger. *Script supervisor:* Marilyn Giardino. *Camera operator:* Marcel Shayne. *Assistant editor:* Courtney V. Hazell. *Set decorator:* Bruce David Weintraub. *Set artist:* Pamela Gray. *Special effects:* Edward Bash. *Title poster art:* Peter Diaferia. *Titles:* Arthur Eckstein. *Stills:* Morgan Renard. *Dance music:* Louis St. Louis. *Songs:* "The Wild Party," "Funny Man," "Not That Queenie of Mine," "Singapore Sally," "Herbert Hoover Drag," "Ain't Nothing Bad About Feeling Good," "Sunday Morning Blues" by Walter Marks. *Choreography:* Patricia Birch. *Costumes:* (Raquel Welch) Ron Talsky; (James Coco, Perry King, David Dukes) Ralph Lauren; (Jennifer Lee, Dena Dietrich, Tiffany Bolling) Ronald Kolodgie; (wardrobe) Eric Kjemvik. *Makeup:* Louis Lane. *Hairstyles:* John Malone. *Sound Editor:* Mary Brown. *Sound recording:* Gary Alper. *Sound re-recording:* Richard Vorisek. *Stunt coordinator:* Teri McComas.
Cast: James Coco (Jolly Grimm), Raquel Welch (Queenie), Perry King (Dale Sword), Tiffany Bolling (Kate), David Dukes (James Morrison), Royal Dano (Tex, Jolly's chauffeur), Dena Dietrich (Mrs. Murchison), Regis J. Cordic (Mr. Murchison), Jennifer Lee (Madeleine True), Marya Small (Bertha), Bobo Lewis (Wilma), Annette Ferra (Nadine),

Eddie Laurence (Kreutzer), Tony Paxton (Sergeant), Waldo K. Berns (Policeman), Nina Faso (Lady in Black), Baruch Lumet (Tailor), Martin Kove (Editor), Ralph Manza (Fruit Dealer), Lark Geib (Rosa), Frederick Franklyn (Sam), J. S. Johnson (Morris), Michael Grant Hall (Oscar D'Armano), Skipper (Phil D'Armano), Don De Natale (Jackie, the Apache Dancer), Tom Reese (Eddy), Geraldine Baron (Grace), Jill Giraldi (Crippled Girl), Barbara Quinn (Mildred), Gloria Godhoke (Redhead), Clea Ariel, Susan Arnold, Joe Arrowsmith, Jonathan Becker, Walter K. Berns, Bob Buckingham, Jennifer Chessman, Mark David Jacobson, Rick Kanter, Kevin Matthews, Luke Matthiessen, Gordon Maus, Bill Merickel, Tony Paxton, Anthony Pecoraro, Jack Sachs, Carmen Savieros, Mark Swope, Ayesha Taft, and Whitney Tower (Party Guests).
Running time: 100 minutes. Movielab color. *Shot on location:* Riverside, California. May–June 1974.
First shown in director's original version: Nice International Book Fair, Nice, France. May 1976.

SWEET SOUNDS

Merchant Ivory Productions. *Director:* Richard Robbins. *Producer:* Ismail Merchant. *Script:* Richard Robbins. *Photography:* Richard Inman Pearce, Fred Murphy. *Music:* Hai-Kung Suh (piano); Herbert Levine, Paul Twerdowsky (guitar); Nanette Levi (violin); Eugenie Dengel (viola); William Hanny (cello). *Editor:* Humphrey Dixon. *Continuity:* Dorothea Swope. *Sound recording:* Larry Loewinger. *Production crew:* Marc Rogers, Roger Dean, John Kelley.
Cast: Teachers: Jean Whitlock, Laura Wilson. Soloists: John Desser, cello; Hai-Kyung Suh, piano. Children: Anna Arimborgo, Adam Cole, Alice Damreau, Ivan Rivera, Ann Sachs, Ronald Sumpter, Andrew Wallerstein, Stash Werner, Yared Williams.
Running time: 29 minutes. Color. *Shot on location:* Mannes College of Music, New York City. July 1976.
Premiered: New York Film Festival. October 1976.

ROSELAND

Merchant Ivory Productions, in association with the Oregon Four. *Director:* James Ivory. *Producer:* Ismail Merchant. *Screenplay:* Ruth Prawer Jhabvala. *Photography:* Ernest Vincze. *Editors:* Humphrey Dixon, Richard Schmiechen. *Music arranger/director:* Michael Gibson. *Executive producers:* Michael T. Murphy, Ottomar Rudolf. *Associate producers:* Dennis J. Murphy, Macy Wall. *Production coordinator:* Lisa Harris. *Production manager:* Jeff Bricmont. *Assistant directors:* David Appleton, Ted Devlin. *Songs:* "Rocking Chair" by

Hoagy Carmichael; "Baubles, Bangles and Beads," "Stranger in Paradise" by Robert Wright, George Forrest; "The Moon and Manakoora" by Frank Loesser, Alfred Newman; "On a Slow Boat to China" by Frank Loesser; "Super Cool" by Elton John, Bernie Taupin, performed by Cheryl Lynn. *Costumes:* Diane Finn Chapman. *Casting:* Judy Abbott. *Dance director:* Patricia Birch. *Titles:* R. Greenberg Associates. *Sound recording:* Cabell Smith. *Sound re-recording:* Jack Higgins. *Sound effects:* Jill Demby. *Production assistants:* Mark Potter, Jr., Janet E. Fishman, Debbie Cohen, Chris Adler, Julia Keydel, Richard Numeroff, Wiley Wood, Mark David Jacobson.
Cast: "The Waltz"—Teresa Wright (May), Lou Jacobi (Stan), Don De Natale (Master of Ceremonies), Louise Kirkland (Ruby), Hetty Galen (Red-Haired Lady), Carol Culver (Young May), Denny Shearer (Eddie); "The Hustle"—Geraldine Chaplin (Marilyn), Helen Gallagher (Cleo), Joan Copeland (Pauline), Christopher Walken (Russell), Conrad Janis (George), Jayne Heller (Bella), Annette Rivera and Floyd Chisholm (Hustle couple), Jeanmarie Evans (Cloakroom Attendant); "The Peabody"—Lilia Skala (Rosa), David Thomas (Arthur), Edward Kogan (Bartender), Madeline Lee (Camille), Stan Rubin (Bert), Dortha Duckworth (Ladies' Room Attendant).
Running time: 104 minutes. Movielab color. *Filmed on location:* New York City. January–February, and April 1977.
World Premiere: New York Film Festival. October 1977.

HULLABALOO OVER GEORGIE AND BONNIE'S PICTURES

Merchant Ivory Productions. For London Weekend Television. *Director:* James Ivory. *Producer:* Ismail Merchant. *Screenplay:* Ruth Prawer Jhabvala. *Photography:* Walter Lassally. *Music:* Vic Flick. *Editor:* Humphrey Dixon. *Sets:* Bansi Chandragupta. *Executive producer:* Melvyn Bragg. *Associate producers:* Nick Young, Vijay Amarani. *Assistants to the director:* Javed Siddique and Prashant Gupta. *Poem:* "Waillie Waillie" (anon.) recited by Jenny Beavan. *Costumes:* Jenny Beavan, Purnima Agarwal. *Makeup:* Mohamed Amir. *Sound recording:* Bob Bentley. *Sound re-recording:* Tony Anscombe.
Cast: Peggy Ashcroft (Lady Gwyneth McLaren Pugh, known as Lady Gee), Larry Pine (Clark Haven), Saeed Jaffrey (Shri Narain), Victor Banerjee (the Maharaja of Tasveer, known as "Georgie"), Aparna Sen (the Maharani of Timarpur, known as "Bonnie"), Jane Booker (Lynn/Joyful Girl), Shamsuddin (Deaf-Mute), Jenny Beavan (Governess), Aladdin Langa (Servant), the choir of

the Sacred Heart of St. Mary's, Jodhpur. *Running time:* 83 minutes. Color. *Shot on location:* Jodhpur, February 1978. *First broadcast:* "The South Bank Show," London Weekend Television. September 1978.

THE EUROPEANS

Merchant Ivory Productions, with the National Film Finance Corporation. *Director:* James Ivory. *Producer:* Ismail Merchant. *Screenplay:* Ruth Prawer Jhabvala, based on the novel by Henry James. *Photography:* Larry Pizer. *Music:* Richard Robbins. *Editor:* Humphrey Dixon. *Art direction:* Jeremiah Rusconi. *Costumes:* Judy Moorcroft. *Associate producer:* Connie Kaiserman. *Production manager:* Joyce Herlihy. *Location manager:* Peter Kean. *Assistant directors:* Jim Maniolas, Christine Fox. *Assistant editor:* Mark Potter, Jr. *Music director/arranger:* Vic Flick. Trio, Opus 17, by Clara Schumann; "Deutsche Tanz," Opus 33, No. 7, by Franz Schubert; "Schomberg Gallop," by G. W. E. Friedrich; "Waltz" from *La Traviata* by Giuseppe Verdi; "Old Folks Quadrilles," "French Quadrilles" by Stephen Foster; "Simple Gifts" traditional Shaker hymn; "Beautiful River" by Robert Lowry. *Choreography:* Elizabeth Aldrich, Charles Garth. *Casting:* Judy Abbott. *Makeup:* Jeanne Richmond, Marianne Grigg. *Title art:* Mark Potter, Sr., Trevor Bond. *Titles:* Hillsberg & Meyer. *Sound:* Derek Ball. *Sound editor:* Brian Blamey. *Sound re-recording:* Doug Turner, Bob Jones. *Production assistants:* Michael Fields, Walter Bursiel, Ellen Dinerstein, Anthony Chase, Karen Shashoua, Steve Bach, John Rusconi. *Cast:* Lee Remick (Eugenia, Baroness Münster), Robin Ellis (Robert Acton), Tim Woodward (Felix), Wesley Addy (Mr. Wentworth), Lisa Eichhorn (Gertrude Wentworth), Nancy New (Charlotte Wentworth), Tim Choate (Clifford Wentworth), Kristan Griffith (Lizzie Acton), Helen Stenborg (Mrs. Acton), Norman Snow (Mr. Brand), Gedda Petry (Augustine). *Running time:* 89 minutes. Color. *Filmed on location:* New Ipswich, New Hampshire, and Salem, Massachusetts, October–November 1978. *World premiere:* Cannes Film Festival. May 1979.

THE FIVE FORTY-EIGHT

Channel 13, New York. *Director:* James Ivory. *Producer:* Peter Weinberg. *Screenplay:* Terrence McNally, based on the story by John Cheever. *Photography:* Andrzej Bartkowiak. *Editor:* David E. McKenna. *Art director:* John Wright Stevens. *Costumes:* Julie Weiss. *Executive producer:* Jac Venza. *Associate producer:* Steve Fairchild. *Production manager:* Joan Clancy. *Location coordinator:* Susie Simons. *Assistant direc-tor:* David Appleton. *Casting:* Howard Feuer. *Makeup:* Arlette Greenfield. *Hairdresser:* Joe Tubens. *Cast:* Laurence Luckinbill (John Blake), Mary Beth Hurt (Jane Dent), Laurinda Barrett (Louise Blake), John DeVries (Henry Watkins), Robert Hitt (Price), Ann McDonough (June Thorpe), Philip Scher (Charlie Blake), Kathy Keeney (Virginia Blake), Nicholas Luckinbill (Tad Watkins), John Harkins (Trace Beardon). *Running time:* 58 minutes. Color. *Filmed on location:* New York City, Massachusetts, New Jersey. August 1979. *First broadcast:* Channel 13, New York City, "Great Performances" series. November 1979.

JANE AUSTEN IN MANHATTAN

Merchant Ivory Productions, in association with Polytel International. *Director:* James Ivory. *Producer:* Ismail Merchant. *Screenplay:* Ruth Prawer Jhabvala. Libretto of *Sir Charles Grandison* by Jane Austen, Samuel Richardson. *Photography:* Ernest Vincze; (opera sequence) Larry Pizer. *Music:* Richard Robbins. *Editor:* David E. McKenna. *Art director:* Jeremiah Rusconi. *Stage settings:* Michael Yeargan. *Costumes:* Jenny Beavan. *Associate producer:* Connie Kaiserman. *Production coordinator:* Wendy Glickstein. *Production manager:* Ronald Palazzo. *Location manager:* Susie Simons. Pierre's work-shop sequences directed by Andrei Serban. *Assistant directors:* Ronald Palazzo, Janet Fishman. *Camera operator:* Don Sweeney. *Songs:* "It's Alright," "Stay Beside Me" by and performed on the guitar by Katrina Hodiak; "Here We Are Again" by Carmine Stippo, per-formed by Kurt Johnson. Opera Singers—(soprano) Jane Bryden, (mezzo) Joyce Andrew, (tenor) Frank Offmeister, (bass) David Evitts. *Casting:* Judy Abbott. *Choreography:* Michael Shawn. *Makeup:* Jeanne Richmond. *Title design:* Hillsberg & Meyer. *Sound:* Cabell Smith; (music) Media Sound. *Sound re-recording:* Jack Higgins. *Jack-of-all-trades:* Mark Potter, Jr. *Production assistants:* Walter Hunnewell, Roger Barrera, Rajeev Talwani, Stephen Dembitzer. *Cast:* Anne Baxter (Lilianna Zorska), Robert Powell (Pierre), Michael Wager (George Midash), Tim Choate (Jamie), John Guerrasio (Gregory), Katrina Hodiak (Katya), Kurt Johnson (Victor), Philip Linkowsky (Fritz), Charles McCaughan (Billy), Nancy New (Jenny), Sean Young (Ariadne), Bernard Barrow (Polson), Lee Doyle (Jarvis), Bella Jarrett (Klein), Naomi Riordan (Mrs. Polson), David Redden (Auctioneer), Gael Ham-mer and Peter McPherson (Unsuccessful Bidders), John Boyle and Tim Burke (Chair Carriers), Iman (Sufi Leader),

Brenda Holmes, Michon Peacock and Christina Stolberg (Dancers), Michael Shawn (Choreographer), Susan Hovey (Marianne), Sarallen (Fairbanks), Jac-quelyn Roberts (Miss Auberry), Sandra Seacat (Thrift-Shop Lady), James Raitt (Pianist), Wayne Tuthill (Clergyman's Clerk). *Running time:* 111 minutes. Movielab color. *Filmed on location:* New York City, Albany, Cohoes (New York). January–March 1980. *First broadcast:* "South Bank Show," London Weekend Television. July 1980.

QUARTET

Merchant Ivory Productions/Lyric Inter-national (Paris). *Director:* James Ivory. *Producers:* Ismail Merchant, Jean-Pierre Mahot de la Querantonnais. *Screenplay:* Ruth Prawer Jhabvala, based on the novel by Jean Rhys. *Photography:* Pierre Lhomme. *Music:* Richard Robbins. *Editor:* Humphrey Dixon. *Art director:* Jean-Jacques Caziot. *Costumes:* Judy Moorcroft. *Executive producer:* Hubert Niogret. *Associate producers:* Humbert Balsan, Connie Kaiserman. *Production controller:* Alain Depardieu. *Location scout:* Jacques Quinternet. *Assistant director:* Hughes de Laugardière. *French dialogue:* Michel Maingois. *Camera operator:* Philippe Brun. *Set dresser:* Robert Christides. *Portraits:* Jean de Gramont, Francois Marcepoil. *Assistant editor:* Mark Potter, Jr. *Editing assis-tant:* Angélique Armand-Delille. *Music extracts:* "Arabesque Valsante" by Mis-cha Levitsky. *Songs:* "The 509," "Full-time Lover" arranged by Luther Hender-son, performed by Armelia McQueen; "Pars" by Jean Lenois, performed by Isabelle Adjani; "L'Air des bijoux" by Boris Gounod, performed by Sophie de Segur. *Music director/arranger:* Vic Flick. *Choreography:* Elizabeth Ald-ridge. *Makeup:* Kenneth Lintott, Tommy Manderson. *Sound editor:* David Renton. *Sound recording:* Bernard Bats. *Music recording:* John Richards. *Sound re-recording:* Richard King. *Sound assis-tant:* Alan Coddington. *English subti-tles:* Titra-Film. *Cast:* Isabelle Adjani (Marya Zelli), Anthony Higgins (Stefan Zelli), Maggie Smith (Lois Heidler), Alan Bates (H. J. Heidler), Pierre Clémenti (Théo, the Pornographer), Daniel Mesguich (Pierre Schlamovitz), Virginia Thevenet (Mlle. Chardin), Suzanne Fflon (Mme. Hautchamp), Sebastien Floche (M. Hautchamp), Sheila Gish (Anna), Daniel Chatto (Guy), Paulita Sedgwick (Esther), Bernice Stegers (Miss Nicholson), Isa-belle Canto Da Maya ("Cri-Cri"), Fran-çois Viaur (Lefranc), Wiley Wood (Cairn), Dino Zanghi, Michael Such and Jean-Pierre Dravel (Prison Guards), Annie Noël (Maid), Maurice Ribot (Pia-nist), Pierre Julien (Impresario), Hum-bert Balsan (Impresario's Friend), Serge

Marquand (Nightclub Owner), Armelia McQueen (Nightclub Singer), Muriel Montose (Marjorie), Caroline Loeb ("Nun"), Jeffrey Kime (James), Shirley Allan (Adriana), Anne-Marie Brissonière, Marie-France de Bourges and Brigitte Hermetz (Les Oiseaux), Joceline Comellas (Café Patronne), Romain Bremond (Youth), Arlette Spetelbroot (Drowned Girl). Monique Mauclair (Hotel Concierge).
Running time: 101 minutes. GTC color. *Filmed on location:* Paris and environs. October–December 1980, March 1981. *World premiere:* Cannes Film Festival. May 1981. *Winner of* Award for Best Actress to Isabelle Adjani.

THE COURTESANS OF BOMBAY

Merchant Ivory Productions, for Channel 4 (London). *Director:* Ismail Merchant. *Producer:* Ismail Merchant. Devised by Ismail Merchant, James Ivory, and Ruth Prawer Jhabvala. *Photography:* Vishnu Mathur. *Editor:* Amit Bose. *Associate producers:* Kareem Samar Wahid Chowhan. *Assistant director:* Michael Fields. *Second unit cameraman:* Rajesh Joshi. *Assistant cameraman:* Gyanchand Rikki. *Co-editor:* Rita Stern. *Assistant editors:* Anna Ksiezopolska, Julie Talen, Dilip Roy. *Titles:* Camera Effects. *Sound recording:* Ray Beckett. *Sound re-recording:* Richard King. *Assistant to director:* Aamer Hussein.
Cast: Saeed Jaffrey, Zohra Segal, Kareem Samar, the performers and the people of Pavan Pool.
Running time: 73 minutes. Color. *Filmed on location:* Bombay, Safipur (U. P.). January, February, December 1981; January–April, September 1982.
Released by Contemporary Films. Academy Cinema, London. January 1983.

HEAT AND DUST

Merchant Ivory Productions. *Director:* James Ivory. *Producer:* Ismail Merchant. *Screenplay:* Ruth Prawer Jhabvala, based on her novel. *Photography:* Walter Lassally. *Music/Music director:* Richard Robbins. *Associate music director:* Zakir Hussain. *Editor:* Humphrey Dixon. *Production designer:* Wilfred Shingleton. *Art directors:* Maurice Fowler and Ram Yadekar. *Costumes:* Barbara Lane. *Associate producers:* Rita Mangat, Connie Kaiserman. *Assistant to producer:* Paul Bradley. *Production coordinator:* Shama Habibullah. *Production manager:* Peter Manley. *Location manager:* Deepak Nayar. *Assistant directors:* Kevan Barker, David Nichols, Gopal Ram. *Urdu dialogue:* Saeed Jaffrey. *Hindi dialogue:* Harish Khare. *Continuity:* Jane Buck. *Camera assistants:* Tony Garrett, Rajesh Joshi. *Assistant editor:* Mark Potter, Jr. *Set dresser:* Agnes Fernandes. *Props:* Tom Freeman. *Stills:* Christopher Cormack. *Musicians:* Pandit Chaurasia

(flute), Sultan Khan (sarangi), Nishat Khan (sitar), Zakir Hussain (percussion), Michael Reeves (piano), Mick Parker (synthesizer), Ameer Mohammed Khan (singer), Harry Rabinowitz (conductor). *Casting director:* Susie Figgis. *Costume assistant:* Mary Ellis. *Makeup:* Gordon Kay. *Makeup assistant:* Mohammed Amir. *Hairdresser:* Carol Hemming. *Assistant hairdresser:* Jeffrey Haines. *Titles:* Camera Effects. *Title art:* Courtesy of Eyre & Hobhouse. *Sound editor:* Brian Blamey. *Assistant sound editor:* Tony Bray. *Sound recording:* Ray Beckett. *Sound re-recording:* Richard King. *Assistant to director:* Prashant Gupta. *Production assistants:* Nancy Vanden Bergh, Piyush Patel.
Cast: (The 1920s: In the Civil Lines at Satipur) Christopher Cazenove (Douglas Rivers), Greta Scacchi (Olivia), Julian Glover (Mr. Crawford), Susan Fleetwood (Mrs. Crawford), Patrick Godfrey (Dr. Saunders), Jennifer Kendal (Mrs. Saunders). (At the Palace in Khatm) Shashi Kapoor (the Nawab), Madhur Jaffrey (the Begum), Nickolas Grace (Harry), Barry Foster (Major Minnies), Amanda Walker (Lady Mackleworth), Sudha Chopra (Chief Princess), Sajid Khan (Dacoit Chief), Daniel Chatto (Guy). (The 1980s: in Satipur town) Julie Christie (Anne), Zakir Hussain (Inder Lal), Ratna Pathak (Rita, Inder Lal's wife), Tarla Mehta (Inder Lal's mother), Charles McCaughan (Chidananda), Praveen Paul (Maji), Jayant Kripalani (Dr. Gopal), Leelabhai (Leelavati).
Running time: 130 minutes. Color. *Filmed on location:* Hyderabad, Gulmarg (Kashmir), London. February–April, August 1982.
Released by Curzon/Enterprise. Curzon Cinema, Mayfair, London. February 1983.

THE BOSTONIANS

Merchant Ivory Productions. In association with WGBH, Boston; Redifussion Films, London; Almi Entertainment Finance Corporation. *Director:* James Ivory. *Producer:* Ismail Merchant. *Screenplay:* Ruth Prawer Jhabvala, based on the novel by Henry James. *Photography:* Walter Lassally. *Music:* Richard Robbins. *Editors:* Katherine Wenning and Mark Potter, Jr. *Production designer:* Leo Austin. *Art directors:* Tom Walden and Don Carpentier. *Costumes:* Jenny Beavan and John Bright. *Executive producers:* Al Schwartz, Michael Landes. *Associate producers:* Connie Kaiserman, Paul Bradley. *Assistant to the producer:* Bill O'Connell. *Production coordinator:* Lorraine Goodman. *Production manager:* Ted Morley. *Location manager:* Alex Decker. *Location coordinator:* Lisa Strout. *Assistant directors:* David Appleton, Ron Peck, Simon Moseley. *Camera assistants:* Tom Paul Hoppe, Bill Floyd. *Set decorator:* Richard Elton. *Scenic artists:* Debbie Davis, Timothy Freuh, Janet Low, Pat Tanpone, Nan Starr, Jon Moynihan, Peter Derbyshire, John Campbell. *Music director:* Harry Rabinowitz. *Music performed by:* (alto) Helen Attfield, (fiddle) Graham Prescott, (organ soloists) David Beyer, Nigel Allcoat. Music Extract—*Lohengrin* (Act 1, Prelude), by Richard Wagner, performed by the Vienna Philharmonic conducted by Rudolph Kempe. *Costume coordinator:* William Pierce. *Makeup:* Jeanne Richmond. *Titles/opticals:* Camera Effects. *Sound editor:* Brian Blamey. *Sound recording:* Ray Beckett; (music) Alan Snelling, (organ) Scott Kein. Dolby Stereo. *Sound re-recording:* Jon Blunt. *Production assistants:* Hadi Zarbafi, Randy Craig, Tom Ehrenfield, David Kimball, Dorothy Berman, Nicola Robinson, Stephen Dembitzer.
Cast: Christopher Reeve (Basil Ransom), Vanessa Redgrave (Olive Chancellor), Madeleine Potter (Verena Tarrant), Jessica Tandy (Miss Birdseye), Nancy Marchand (Mrs. Burrage), Wesley Addy (Dr. Tarrant), Barbara Bryne (Mrs. Tarrant), Linda Hunt (Dr. Prance), Nancy New (Mrs. Luna), Charles McCaughan (Music Hall Policeman), John Van Ness Philip (Henry Burrage), Wallace Shawn (Mr. Pardon), Maura Moynihan (Henrietta Stackpole), Martha Farrar (Mrs. Farrinder), Peter Bogyo (Mr. Gracie), Dusty Maxwell (Newton), Lee Doyle (Mr. Filer), J. Lee Morgan (Music Hall Official), Dee French (Patient), Jane Manners (Maid), Janet Cicchese (Irish Washerwoman), Scott Kradolfer (Tough Boy).
Running time: 122 minutes. Color. *Filmed on location:* Newport, Rhode Island; Boston; Martha's Vineyard; New York City; Troy, New York; London. August–October 1983, March 1984. *World premiere:* Cannes Film Festival, 1984. Director's Fortnight.

A ROOM WITH A VIEW

Merchant Ivory Productions. *Director:* James Ivory. *Producer:* Ismail Merchant. *Screenplay:* Ruth Prawer Jhabvala, based on the novel by E. M. Forster. *Photography:* Tony Pierce-Roberts. *Music:* Richard Robbins. *Editor:* Humphrey Dixon. *Production designers:* (Italy) Gianni Quaranta, (England) Brian Ackland-Snow. *Art directors:* Brian Savegar and Elio Altamura. *Costumes:* (design) Jenny Beavan and John Bright, (coordinator) William Pierce, (supervisor) Brenda Dabbs. *Associate producers:* Paul Bradley, (Italy) Peter Marangoni. *Production coordinator:* Caroline Hill. *Production managers:* Ann Wingate, Lanfranco Diotallevi. *Location manager:* (England) Jilly Gutterridge. *Assistant directors:* Kevan Barker, Pippo Pischotto, Daniel Sonnis, Simon Moseley. *Second unit photographer:* Sergio Melaranci. *Set dressers:*

Floriano Porzionato, Dennis Simmonds, Mick Flanders. *Music Extracts:* "O mio babbino caro" from *Gianni Schicchi*, "Chi il bel sogno di Doretta" from *La Rondine* by Giacomo Puccini, performed by Kiri Te Kanawa, the London Philharmonic Orchestra, conducted by Sir John Pritchard; "Mademoiselle Modiste" by Victor Herbert, performed by The Dryden Orchestra of the Eastman School of Music. *Music direction/orchestrations:* Francis Shaw, Barrie Guard. *Music production:* Simon Heyworth. *Casting director:* Celestia Fox. *Wardrobe superintendents:* Sally Turner, William Pierce. *Makeup:* Christine Beveridge. *Title design:* Chris Allies. *Title backgrounds:* Folco Cianfanelli. *Sound editors:* Tony Lenny, Peter Compton, Alan Killick. *Sound recording:* Ray Beckett; (music) Brian Masterson (Windmill Lane Studios, Dublin). Dolby Stereo. *Sound re-recording:* Richard King (Worldwide Sound). *Italian revoicing:* Dino Colizzi. *Production assistants:* Andrew Bergen, Daniele Nepi, Nayeem Hafiska, Paul Scacchi, Carlo Mantegazza, Elizabeth Swisher, Jane Delandro, Stephen Dembitzer.
Cast: Maggie Smith (Charlotte Bartlett), Helena Bonham Carter (Lucy Honeychurch), Denholm Elliott (Mr. Emerson), Julian Sands (George Emerson), Daniel Day Lewis (Cecil Vyse), Simon Callow (Reverend Arthur Beebe), Judi Dench (Miss Eleanor Lavish), Rosemary Leach (Mrs. Honeychurch), Rupert Graves (Freddy Honeychurch), Patrick Godfrey (Mr. Eager), Fabia Drake (Catharine Alan), Joan Henley (Teresa Alan), Maria Britneva (Mrs. Vyse), Amanda Walker (Cockney Signora), Peter Cellier (Sir Harry Otway), Mia Fothergill (Minnie Beebe), Patricia Lawrence (Mrs. Butterworth), Miro Guidelli (Santa Croce Guide), Mattelock Gibbs and Kitty Aldridge (the New Charlotte and Lucy), Freddy Korner (Mr. Ffloyd), Elizabeth Marangoni (Miss Pole), Lucca Rossi (Phaeton), Isabella Celani (Persephone), Luigi Di Fiori (Murdered Youth).
Running time: 117 minutes. Technicolor. *Filmed on location:* Florence, Kent, London. May–July 1985. *Released by* Cinecom; Paris Cinema, New York City. March 1986.

MAURICE

Merchant Ivory Productions. *Director:* James Ivory. *Producer:* Ismail Merchant. *Screenplay:* Kit Hesketh-Harvey and James Ivory. *Photography:* Pierre Lhomme. *Music:* Richard Robbins. *Editor:* Katherine Wenning. *Production designer:* Brian Ackland-Snow. *Art director:* Peter James. *Costumes:* Jenny Beavan and John Bright. *Associate producer:* Paul Bradley. *Production supervisor:* Raymond Day. *Production accountants:* William Tyler and Sunil

Kirparam. *Production coordinator:* Joyce Turner. *Assistant director:* Michael Zimbrich. *Continuity:* Lorely Farley. *Camera operators:* Nigel Willoughby and Tony Woodcock. *Assistant editor:* Andrew Marcus. *Makeup:* Mary Hillman. *Hairdresser:* Carol Hemming. *Casting director:* Celestia Fox. *Stills photographers:* Jon Gardey and Katya Grenfell. *Location scout:* Joe Friedman. *Location managers:* Maggie Parsons and Natasha Grenfell. *Sound editor:* Tony Lenny.
Cast: James Wilby (Maurice), Hugh Grant (Clive), Rupert Graves (Alec), Denholm Elliott (Dr. Barry), Simon Callow (Mr. Ducie), Billie Whitelaw (Mrs. Hall), Ben Kingsley (Lasker-Jones), Judy Parfitt (Mrs. Durham), Phoebe Nichols (Anne Durham), Mark Tandy (Risley), Helena Michell (Ada Hall), Kitty Aldridge (Kitty Hall), Patrick Godfrey (Simcox), Michael Jenn (Archie), Barry Foster (Dean Cornwallis), Peter Eyre (Mr. Borenius), Catherine Rabett (Pippa Durham), Orlando Wells (Young Maurice).
Running time: 135 minutes. *Filmed on location:* Wilbury Park, Wiltshire; King's College, Cambridge; London; Gloucester. October–December 1986, May 1987.
World premiere: Venice Film Festival. August 1987. *Winner of* Silver Lion for Best Director; Award for Best Actor shared by James Wilby and Hugh Grant; Best Music: Richard Robbins.

THE DECEIVERS

Merchant Ivory Productions. *Director:* Nicholas Meyer. *Producer:* Ismail Merchant. *Screenplay:* Michael Hirst, from the novel by John Masters. *Photography:* Walter Lassally. *Music:* John Scott. *Editor:* Richard Trevor. *Art directors:* Gianfranco Fumagalli and Ram Yedekar. *Production designer:* Ken Adam. *Costumes:* Jenny Beavan and John Bright. *Executive producer:* Michael White. *Coproducer:* Tim Van Rellim. *Associate producer:* Leon Falk. *Production supervisor:* Anthony Waye. *Production manager:* Deepak Nayar. *Production accountants:* Alex Matcham and Sunil Kirparam. *Production coordinators:* Dena Vincent and Eleanor Chaudhuri. *Assistant directors:* Chris Carreras and Shah Jehan. *Camera operator:* Tony Woodcock. *Makeup:* Gordon Kay. *Hairdresser:* Vera Mitchell. *Casting directors:* Celestia Fox (U.K.) and Jennifer Jaffrey (India). *Stills photographer:* Mikki Ansin. *Location manager:* R. P. Sondhi. *Sound editor:* Jonathan Bates. *Sound recordist:* Claude Hitchcock.
Cast: Pierce Brosnan (William Savage), Saeed Jaffrey (Hussein), Shashi Kapoor (Chandra Singh), Helena Michell (Sarah Wilson), Keith Michell (Colonel Wilson), David Robb (George Angelsmith), Tariq Yunus (Feringea), Julal

Agha (Nawab), Gary Cady (Lieutenant Maunsell), Salim Ghouse (Piroo), Neena Gupta (Widow), Nayeem Hafizka (Sepoy), Bijoya Jena (Harlot), H. N. Kalla (Nawab's Servant), Kammo (Official), Goga Kapoor (Sher Dil), Manmohan Krishna (Old Rajput), Harish Magon (Sepoy), Manmaujee (Ferryman), Giles Masters (Captain Devril), Ramesh Ranga (Rajput's Son), Dilip Singh Rathore (Sowar), Hilla Sethna (Chandra Singh's Maidservant), R. P. Sondhi (Prisoner), Kanwaljit (Gopal), Shanmukha Scrinivas (Hira Lal), Dalip Tahil (Daffadar Ganesha), Tim Van Rellim (Reverend Matthias), Rajesh Vivek (Priest), Amin, Akbar Bakshi, Ramesh Goyal, Kaushel, Haroon Khan, Nilesh Malhotra (Thugs).
Running time: 113 minutes. Color. *Filmed on location:* Jaipur, Khajuraho, India. September–November 1987. *Released by* Curzon/Enterprise. Odeon Haymarket Theatre, London. September 1988.

SLAVES OF NEW YORK

Merchant Ivory Productions, for Tri-Star Pictures. *Director:* James Ivory. *Producers:* Ismail Merchant and Gary Hendler. *Screenplay:* Tama Janowitz, based on her collection of stories. *Photography:* Tony Pierce-Roberts. *Music:* Richard Robbins. *Editor:* Katherine Wenning. *Production design:* David Gropman. *Art director:* Karen Schulz. *Costumes:* Carol Ramsey. *Associate producers:* Fred Hughes and Vincent Fremont. *Production manager:* Mary Kane. *First assistant director:* Richard Hawley. *Second assistant director:* Timothy Lonsdale. *First assistant cameraman:* Jeff Tufano. *Second assistant cameraman:* Robin Brown. *Associate editor:* Andrew Marcus. *Assistant editor:* Kate MacDonald. *Songs:* "Mother Dearest," performed by Joe Leeway; "Say Hi To Your Guy," performed by Johan Carlo and Michael Butler; "Some Guys Have All the Luck," performed by Maxi Priest; "Tumblin' Down," performed by Ziggy Marley and the Melody Makers; "Admit It" and "Love Overlap," performed by Ambitious Lovers; "Buffalo Stance," performed by Neneh Cherry; "Girlfriend," performed by Boy George; "Change Your Mind," performed by Camper Von Beethoven; "Good Life," performed by Inner City; "Fall in Love With Me," performed by Iggy Pop; "Tongue Dance," performed by Les Rita Mitsouko. Additional Music: "Warrior," "Am I Blue?," "Dad, I'm in Jail," "Grand Tour," "Glück Das Mir Verlieb," "Love Is Like An Itching In My Heart," "I Need A Man," "O Ruddier Than the Cherry." *Makeup:* Marilyn Carbone. *Hairdresser:* Anthony Sorrentino. *Sound editor:* Dan Sable. *Assistant sound editor:* Lynn Sable. *Sound re-recording:* Lee Dichter. *Casting:* Howard Feuer.

Cast: Bernadette Peters (Eleanor), Adam Coleman Howard (Stash), Chris Sarandon (Victor Okrent), Mary Beth Hurt (Ginger Booth), Madeleine Potter (Daria), Nick Corri (Marley Mantello), Charles McCaughan (Sherman McVittie), Mercedes Ruehl (Samantha), Jonas Abry (Mickey), Stephen Bastone (Chauffeur), Denise-Marie Beaumont (Ballerina), Mark Boone, Jr. (Mitch), Diane Brill (Jogger), Steve Buscemi (Wilfredo), Michael Butler (Performance Artist), Richy Canatta (Saxophonist), Johan Carlo (Performance Artist), Betty Comden (Mrs. Wheeler), Anthony Crivello (Hairdresser), Raye Dowell (Cheerleader), Christine Dunford ("B"), Stash Franklin (Graffiti Artist), Kevin John Gee (Kyoshi), Aaron Goodstone (Graffiti Artist), Adam Green (Max), Tammy Grimes (Georgette), Louis Guss (Vardig), Rich Hara (Tetsu), John Harkins (Chuck Dade Dolger), George Harris (Super), Francine Hunter (Hairdresser), Paul Jabara (Derelict), Sakina Jaffrey (Wilfredo's Receptionist), Tama Janowitz (Abby), Anna Katarina (Mooshka), Ken Kensei (Kiochi), Freddy Korner (Party Guest), Anthony La Paglia (Henry), Kim Larese (Ballerina), Jennifer Lee (Polly), Joe Leeway (Johnny Jalouse), Philip Lenkowsky (Fritz), Maura Moynihan (Mona), Harsh Nayyar (Dr. Pandiya), Suzanne O'Neill (Victor's Receptionist), Lazaro Perez (Bill), Dustin Pittman (Party Guest), Paul Potter (Simon St. Simon), Paige Powell (Party Guest), Mark Robinson (Derelict), Stillman Rockefeller (Man Who Points), Michael Schoeffling (Jan), Richard Steinmetz (Party Guest), Michael David Tanney (Toddler), Stanley Tucci (Darryl), Fabio Urana (Vandal), Bruce Peter Young (Mikell).
Running time: 124 minutes. *Filmed on location:* New York City. April–June, September 1988.
First released: Cinema One, New York City. March 1989.

THE PERFECT MURDER

Merchant Ivory Productions. *Director:* Zafar Hai. *Producer:* Wahid Chowhan. *Executive producer:* Ismail Merchant. *Screenplay:* H. R. F. Keating and Zafar Hai, from Keating's novel. *Photography:* Walter Lassally. *Music:* Richard Robbins. *Editor:* Charles Rees. *Art director:* Ram Yadekar. *Costumes:* Sally Turner. *Production coordinator:* Shahnaz Vahanvaty. *Assistant director:* Shahjehan. *Stills photographer:* Sooni Taraporevala. *Sound editors:* Mark Potter, Anna Sheperd, and John Silverberg. *Sound mixer:* Mike Shoring. *Casting director:* Jennifer Jaffrey.
Cast: Nassiruddin Shah (Inspector Ghote), Stellen Skarsgard (Axel Svensson), Dinshaw Daji (Mr. Perfect), Archana Puran Singh (Miss Twinkle), Madhur Jaffrey (Mrs. Lal), Sakeena Jaf-

frey (Neena Lal), Amjad Khan (Lala Heera Lal), Ratna Pathak Shah (Pratima Ghote), Dalip Tahil (Dilip Lal), Baba Majgoakar (Jeweler), Anu Kapoor (Tiny Man), Vijoo Khote (Head Constable), Mohan Agashe (A. C. P. Samaut), Wahid Chowhan (Producer), Vinod Nagpal (Minister), Gopi Krishna (Dance Master), Ashley D'Silva (Photographer), Pearl Padamsee (Nurse), Johnny Walker (Jain), Liliput (Black Shirt), P. M. Maniar (Drunken Guest), Sameer Kakkad (Felix Sousa), Imaaduddin Shah (Ved Ghote), Aida Noorani (Student), Nayeem Hafizka (Prem Lal), Rajesh Vivek (Zero Police), Salim Ghouse (Caste-Marks Goonda), Bomi Kapadia (Sergeant Moos).
Running time: 93 minutes. Color.
Filmed on location: Bombay. January–February 1987.
Released by Curzon/Enterprise. Cannon Cinema, London. June 1988.

MR. AND MRS. BRIDGE

Merchant Ivory Productions/Robert Halmi, for Cineplex Odeon Films. *Director:* James Ivory. *Producer:* Ismail Merchant. *Screenplay:* Ruth Prawer Jhabvala from the novels *Mrs. Bridge* and *Mr. Bridge* by Evan S. Connell. *Photography:* Tony Pierce-Roberts. *Music:* Richard Robbins. *Editor:* Humphrey Dixon. *Art director:* Karen Schulz. *Production design:* David Gropman. *Art director (France):* Régis Des Plas. *Costumes:* Carol Ramsey. *Executive producer:* Robert Halmi. *Associate producer and production manager:* Mary Kane. *Production supervisor:* Donald Rosenfeld. *Associate producer (France):* Humbert Balsan. *Production assistants:* Maggie Murphy and Tina Stauffer. *Assistant director:* David Sardi. *Second assistant director:* Matthew Rowland. *Assistant director (France):* Patrick Delabrière. *Assistant to the director:* Tom Freeman. *First camera assistant:* Jeff Tufano. *Second camera assistant:* Bonnie Blake. *Stills photographer:* Mikki Ansin. *Co-editor:* Andrew Marcus. *Assistant editor:* Kate MacDonald. *Set decorator:* Joyce Gilstrap. *Assistant art director (France):* Rosanna Sacco. *Makeup:* Toy Russell-VanLierop. *Makeup for Paul Newman:* Monty Westmore. *Hairdresser:* Vera Mitchell. *Supervising sound editor:* Robert Hein. *Sound editors:* Tony Martinez and Lori Ben-Yakir. *Re-recording mixer:* Tom Fleischman. *Casting:* Joanna Merlin.
Cast: Paul Newman (Walter Bridge), Joanne Woodward (India Bridge), Blythe Danner (Grace Barron), Simon Callow (Dr. Alex Sauer), Kyra Sedgwick (Ruth Bridge), Robert Sean Leonard (Douglas Bridge), Margaret Welsh (Caroline Bridge), Austin Pendleton (Mr. Gadbury), Saundra McClain (Harriet), Diane Kagan (Julia), Gale Garnett (Mabel Ong), Remak Ramsay (Virgil

Barron), Robert Westenberg (Ruth's boyfriend), John Bell (Douglas Bridge as a boy), Marcus Giamatti (Gil Davis), Robert Levine (Avrum Rhinegold), Addison Myers and Roger Burget (Men at Businessmen's Table), Al Christy (Judge), Joe Tinoco (Plaintiff), Ben Stephenson (Law Clerk), Alison Sneegas (Band Vocalist), Mark Yonally (Youth at High School Dance), Buck Baker (Scoutmaster), Danny Cox (Country Club Steward), Robyn Rosenfeld (Genevieve), Roch Leibovici (Watch Seller on the Quai), Hubert Saint Macary (Copyist in the Louvre), Laurence Goua (Principal Can-Can Dancer), The Nocolodis (Moulin Rouge Tumblers), Judy Judd (First bridge Player), Nora Denny (Second Bridge Player), Charles Perkins, Allen Monroe, Richard Ross, Milton Abel (Jazz Musicians), Spencer Keesee (Couperin), Kathy Quinn-Byrne (Paquita), John Anthony (Rod), Jennifer Conforti (Rod's girl), Tom Hall (Aztec Room Waiter), Joanne Carr (Prison Matron), Florence Hall (The Barrons's Maid), Lee Lambert (Corporal Cipkowski), Jocelyn Hamilton (Florist's Assistant), Anny Knott (Flower Shop Owner), Melissa Newman (Young India at the Pool).
Running time: 125 minutes. *Filmed on location:* Paris; Kansas City, Missouri; Toronto, Ottawa, Canada; New York City. September–November 1989, February 1990.
World premiere: Venice Film Festival. September 1990.

THE BALLAD OF THE SAD CAFE

Merchant Ivory Productions, Angelika Films Release. *Director:* Simon Callow. *Producer:* Ismail Merchant. *Photography:* Walter Lassally. *Screenplay:* Michael Hirst, based on the story by Carson McCullers and the play by Edward Albee. *Music:* Richard Robbins. *Editor:* Andrew Marcus. *Production design:* Bruno Santini. *Executive producer:* Paul Bradley. *Associate producer:* Donald Rosenfeld. *Costume design:* Marianna Elliott. *Casting:* Shirley Rich.
Cast: Vanessa Redgrave (Miss Amelia), Keith Carradine (Marvin Macy), Rod Steiger (Reverend Willin), Cork Hubbert (Cousin Lymon), Austin Pendleton (Lawyer Taylor), Beth Dixon (Mary Hale), Lanny Flaherty (Merlie Ryan), Mert Hatfield (Stumpy McPhail), Earl Hindman (Henry Macy), Anne Pitoniak (Mrs. McPhail), Frederick Johnson (Jeff), Laurie Raymond (Sadie Ricketts), Joe Stephens (Henry Ford Crimp), Keith Wommack (Tom Rainey), Kevin Wommack (George Rainey), Laura Burns (Molly Kelly).
Running time: 100 minutes. *Filmed on location:* Spicewood, Texas. June–August 1990.
World premiere: Berlin Film Festival. February 1991.

Index